International
Library of the
Philosophy of
Education

Beyond
domination

International Library of the Philosophy of Education

General Editor

R. S. Peters

Professor of Philosophy of Education
Institute of Education
University of London

Beyond domination

An essay in the political philosophy of education

Patricia White

Routledge & Kegan Paul

London, Boston, Melbourne and Henley

First published in 1983
by Routledge & Kegan Paul plc
39 Store Street, London WC1E 7DD, England
9 Park Street, Boston, Mass. 02108, USA
296 Beaconsfield Parade, Middle Park,
Melbourne, 3206, Australia
Broadway House, Newtown Road,
Henley-onThames, Oxon RG9 1EN, England
Printed in Great Britain by
Redwood Burn Ltd., Trowbridge, Wiltshire
© Patricia White 1983

Library of Congress Cataloging in Publication Data

White, Patricia, 1937–

   Beyond domination.
   International library of the philosophy of education.
   Bibliography: p.
   Includes index.
   1. School management and organization.   2. Politics
and education.   3. Democracy.   4. Educational law and
legislation.   5. Parent and child (law).   I. Title
II. Series.
LB2805.W476   1983   370'.1   83–9507

ISBN 0–7100–9765–4

To my parents
Reginald Arthur and
Lilian Marian Middle

Contents

Contents

General editor's note

There is a growing interest in philosophy of education amongst students of philosophy as well as amongst those who are more specifically and practically concerned with educational problems. Philosophers, of course, from the time of Plato onwards, have taken an interest in education and have dealt with education in the context of wider concerns about knowledge and the good of life. But it is only quite recently in this country that philosophy of education has come to be conceived of as a specific branch of philosophy like the philosophy of science or political philosophy.

To call philosophy of education a specific branch of philosophy is not, however, to suggest that it is a distinct branch in the sense that it could exist apart from established branches of philosophy such as epistemology, ethics and philosophy of mind. It would be more appropriate to conceive of it as drawing on established branches of philosophy and bringing them together in ways which are relevant to educational issues. In this respect the analogy with political philosophy would be a good one. Thus use can often be made of work that already exists in philosophy. In tackling, for instance, issues such as the rights of parents and children, punishment in schools, and the authority of the teacher, it is possible to draw on and develop work already done by philosophers on 'rights', 'punishment', and 'authority'. In other cases, however, no systematic work exists in the relevant branches of philosophy – e.g. on concepts such as 'education', 'teaching', 'learning', 'indoctrination'. So philosophers of education have had to break new ground – in these cases the philosophy of mind. Work on educational issues can also bring to life and throw new light on long-standing problems in philosophy. Concentration, for instance, on the particular predicament of children can throw new light on problems of punishment and responsibility. G. E. Moore's old worries about what sorts of things are good in themselves can be brought to life by urgent questions about the justification of the curriculum in schools.

There is a danger in philosophy of education, as in any other applied field, of polarization to one of two extremes. The work could be practically relevant but philosophically feeble; or it could be philosophically sophisticated but remote from practical problems. The aim of the new International Library of Philosophy of Education is to build up a body of fundamental work in this area which is both practically relevant and philosophically competent. For unless it achieves both types of objective it will fail to satisfy those for whom it is intended and fall short of the conception of philosophy of education which the International Library is meant to embody.

R.S. Peters

Acknowledgments

I would like first of all to thank the four people from whom I received a basic grounding in the disciplines of educational theory, Basil Bernstein, Paul Hirst, Richard Peters and Roger Wilson. They and their work are very different. What they have in common is that they have shown to generations of students that education matters and that nothing less than the highest standards of argument, analysis and theory construction will do for the critical commentary on educational practice which educational theory should provide.

I would also especially like to thank my husband, John White. Without his continuing support and encouragement over many years this book and the papers which preceded it would never have appeared. More particularly, this would have been a very much less adequate book without the benefit of his careful reading of successive drafts and his philosophical and literary advice. To my daughter, Louise, I owe two debts. I must thank her, first, for enrolling in two successive summer vacations for courses in diving, advanced swimming, tennis, badminton, volley ball, trampolining, gymnastics, golf and football, so that I could be left in peace at my desk. (She is not particularly inclined towards sports.) The second debt is an intellectual one. To Louise I owe many perceptive comments on instances of domination – sexual, generational – which would have escaped me. To her indeed I owe the title.

Thanks are also due to colleagues and students, particularly my research students, past and present, with whom I have discussed many of the ideas in this book.

For a woman in our society with professional and family responsibilities to produce any extended piece of writing, considerable material support behind the scenes is necessary. For unfailingly providing this my thanks to go Ann Denny and Betty Green.

For typing a first draft of parts of this book I would like to thank Oscar Munoz. For typing the final draft and preparing the manuscript for publication I am indebted to Bernadette Cifuentes for a superlative job.

Part of chapter two first appeared in a paper, 'Work-place Democracy and Political Education', in the *Journal of Philosophy of Education*, 13, 1979. Parts of chapter three originally appeared in a paper, 'Political Education and School Organisation', in *Issues for the Eighties: Some Central Questions of Education* edited by Brian Simon and William Taylor, published by Batsford and in a paper, 'Political Education in a Democracy: The Implications for Teacher Education', in the *Journal of Further and Higher Education*, volume 1, no. 3, 1977. Chapter four is a modified version of a paper, 'Democratic Perspectives in the Training of Headteachers', which appeared in the *Oxford Review of Education*, volume 8, no. 1, 1982. I would like to thank the publishers and editors of the book and the journals for permission to use material from those papers, in each case with certain changes and amendments, in this essay.

Introduction

A book with this title, dealing as it does with the political machinery and political education appropriate to a democratic society, might appear to belong to the growing corpus of Marxist, or neo-Marxist, works on education and politics. In one sense, as they say, we are all Marxists now and this essay accepts and uses much of the classical and neo-Marxist critique of contemporary capitalist liberal democracies. The theoretical bases of its recommendations for education in a participatory democracy are not Marxist, however, but in the liberal democratic tradition. While I have drawn on the ideas of Marxists like Gramsci and C.B. Macpherson, much more fundamental has been the work of thinkers like Dworkin, Ackerman, Lukes, Giddens, Carole Pateman and Gutmann. It is these radical liberal thinkers, it seems to me, who have gone furthest in clarifying key issues to do with a democratic society, issues like the nature of power, the proper control of economic power, control of the majority's power and dissent within a democracy.

This essay is unashamedly radical in the use to which it puts much of this work - in curbing the power of teachers, including headteachers, in stripping parents of their rights and in making political education the keystone of education - but it is not Marxist. I stress this because many people appear to believe that there are just two sorts of philosophy of education - either a radical Marxist one or one which serves as an ideological prop to the status quo. But these are not the only possibilities. Recent work in liberal democratic theory is capable both of mounting a fundamental critique of contemporary political and educational practice and of suggesting more defensible alternatives. It is in this latter respect that it has more to offer, I would submit, than any

1

Marxist analysis with which I am familiar.   I cannot be
the only reader of Marxist works on education who finds
much to agree with in their blistering critiques of capitalism but who feels that waiting for the Revolution to
lead us into an ill-defined Utopia is not the most practical of suggestions as to how we can escape our present
troubles. (1)

In its discussion of democracy the book does not remain
at the level of general principles - justice, freedom,
fraternity - but attempts to devise machinery through
which these general principles might be implemented.   In
this respect it bears the marks of American influence and
the considerable work done in political philosophy in the
United States on practical political issues like civil
rights, positive discrimination, a just scale of incomes
and so on.   This type of work has not figured to any
great extent in British philosophy of education.   British
philosophers of education, anxious to make the subject as
respectable as its purer cousins like philosophy of religion or philosophy of science, have often been reluctant
to offer partly empirical claims and recommendations.
Working in a large institution with professional colleagues in other educationally related disciplines, psychology, sociology, economics, etc., has made me see what
an opportunity has been lost by such a purist stance.   If
philosophers do not sometimes trace the institutional and
policy implications of their work, making certain non-
philosophical assumptions, and necessarily sticking their
necks out, it is most unlikely that anyone else will do
so.   If one thinks, therefore, that philosophy of education has important contributions to make to educational
policy-making one has, I believe, to demonstrate this oneself - even at the risk of a little 'impurity'.

This essay is unlike other work in the field because of
its focus on machinery rather than principles.   It is
also different in placing political education at the
centre of education as a whole.   Many writers have
recently lamented the political ignorance and apathy that
exists among young people and have urged us as a society
to do something about it.   What they most often recommend
is that we try to fill the ignorance gap by plugs of political education.   Nothing could be more inappropriate.
Political education provides the context or framework for
the whole of education: it is not in any sense peripheral
or an 'extra'.   This essay does not make the usual modest
claims for political education but a bold one for its cen-
trality.

How does all this concretely translate into chapters?
The first chapter is concerned with the basic principles
and assumptions underlying democracy, their justification,
and why, given an understanding of these principles, the
presumption must be in favour of what has come to be
called a participatory democracy.   Chapter two discusses
the kind of machinery and attitudes which must character-
ise participatory democracy as well as practices and attitudes which are ruled out.   At this point the essay
changes tack.   I consider what kind of educational strategies would be appropriate to help move a society like our
own towards greater democracy.   I suggest in Chapter
three the kind of political education needed by all children as part of their basic education and outline various
policies for teacher training, the curriculum, and research required to realise that education.   Chapter four
is concerned with a crucial role in our current educational system if we are interested in making it more democrat
ic - the role of the headteacher.   I give reasons for
thinking that there will be no such role as we know it in
a fully participatory democracy.   In the transition to
such a system, however, headteachers, with suitable training, can be powerful agents for change.   Chapter four
outlines this strategy and the training involved.   In
Chapter five the role of parents is examined, both in the
fully fledged participatory democracy and in our society.
The claim is made that parents have no independent rights
as parents in respect of their children's education:
whatever rights they have are dependent on their duties.
These duties are fairly extensive and demanding but they
need not prove too onerous, even for single parents,
because they can be complemented by a well-developed
system of community support.   This whole essay is about
power and therefore the possibilities for domination.   It
is common in treatments of power for those with an interest in reducing the power of teachers and the educational
system over students to champion the rights of parents and
give to parents all they have taken away from teachers.
This does little, if anything, to reduce indefensible
exercises of power over young people.   I suggest a whole
pattern of parental duties and community support designed
to control exercises of power in education to enable the
development of autonomous morally responsible citizens.
Chapters three, four and five need to be taken together as
a set of complementary policies.   For solid and even progress towards a participatory democracy the kind of political education outlined and a changed role for parents
are both necessary.   The suggested plan for training programmes for heads is a practical suggestion for moving

educational institutions further along the democratic path
now.

Given its policy orientation, I hope this book will be
read not only by students of philosophy of education but
also by policy-makers and not least by individual teachers
and parents.   I have put forward for critical scrutiny
policies which are implementable at national and local
level as well as ones implementable at school level or in
individual classrooms and homes.   Critical debate amongst
interested parties will reveal whether any of them are, in
whole or in part, worth considering as practical propositions.

Two final topical points.   I am assuming in this essay
a multicultural society whilst being aware that I am not
able to consider all the issues that are raised for democratic principles and practice by a culturally plural
society, given my particular focus of interest here.
Some issues have, however, impinged on my treatment at
various points.   One of the preoccupations of this essay
is, for instance, the position of minorities whether tem-
porary or permanent, and of whatever kind, whether bound
together by a common religious pattern of life or by some
other common interest or tradition.   The majority/minor-
ity problem is one of the most intractable for any democratic community, as this essay shows, but I try to argue
that the participatory democracy is able to cope with this
problem better than most in that, for instance, many
activities and enterprises are devolved to a local level
so that the minority in the national community becomes the
majority in the local one.   In this, and in other ways,
what are often referred to as issues of the multicultural
society are dealt with pari passu.   It would be surprising if this were not so in a conception of democracy which
takes as its starting point the assumption that people
should lead autonomous lives of their own choosing as
morally responsible citizens.

Apart from my stylistic use of 'she' rather than the
conventional 'he' and some brief discussion of sexism in
Chapters three and five, I have not devoted much space to
the position of women within the participatory democracy.
Again the reason is obvious: if the basic framework of
the community is so structured as to allow people to live
out autonomous lives this applies as much to women as to
men and there is no point in arguing the case twice over -
for men and then for women. (2)   I cannot help remarking,
however, that amongst prominent contemporaries working in

the area of democratic theory the best known advocates of
participatory democracy are women.   Considering the very
much smaller number of women working in the field, this is
quite striking. (3)   As a philosopher I have simply dealt
with these ideas in the following chapters regardless of
their provenance.   But perhaps as a conclusion to this
introduction I can allow myself a little speculation on
this phenomenon.   Is it simply coincidence?   My early
sociological training makes me suspicious of such coinci-
dences.   Is it that women are drawn to explore theories
which plan for the control of power so that everyone can
flourish and live autonomous, morally responsible lives,
because, whatever their country or social class they are
likely to have experienced domination in many forms before
they ever get to the stage of writing philosophical books?

1 Democratic principles and basic assumptions

In this chapter I want to make explicit the bedrock principles and assumptions underlying democracy in <u>any</u> society.
In fact of course democratic governments and institutions
will always be situated in particular historical societies
and in the following chapter I want to examine the kinds
of institutions and practices appropriate to realise democratic principles in industrialised societies of the late
twentieth century. The kind of thing I shall be doing in
Chapters two to five - attempting to match institutions in
a particular historical situation to the general principles outlined in this chapter - is, it seems to me, a
task as important as the original formulation and refining
of the principles. It is a task which political philosophers have increasingly been tackling for the twentieth
century - classical political philosophers always did this,
after all - especially in a great burst of publications in
the 1970s. I am thinking particularly of work in the
United States on, for instance, just and unjust wars, just
income policies, children's rights, racism, feminism and
positive discrimination, much of which is represented in
the journal <u>Philosophy and Public Affairs</u>. It is, however, a kind of philosophical work which has not as yet,
as I indicated in my Introduction, made much of a showing
in British philosophy of education. In the general area
of democracy and democratic theory work has tended to
remain at the level of the exposition of general principles. There has been little attempt by philosophers of
education - except perhaps in the area of issues to do
with the democratic control of the curriculum (see, e.g.,
Sockett, 1980) - to attempt to offer suggestions on the
concrete implementation of principles in our particular
historical situation. One might say, of course, that
there is a good reason for this. Philosophy is a matter
of the formulation and refining of concepts and general

6

principles.   It is for someone else to apply these to the
concrete situation.   But who?   Within the educational
field I cannot see any 'detail worker' to whom I could
pass on this job.   In any case the classical political
philosophers did it (cf. Plato on the domestic arrangements for the Guardians, Locke on decision-making machinery and Hegel on the family), American political philosophers tackle these questions, and in the UK there is work
like The Sceptical Feminist (Richards, 1980), which must
surely support the case that there is an important job for
philosophers to do in applying general principles to the
particular situation.   It is of course a messy job in
that one has to make empirical assumptions of all kinds,
any one of which, if false, may destroy one's case.   One
must, however, be robustly prepared for one's work to be
rapidly overtaken and to see this sort of endeavour as a
kind of brainstorming in print.   Its value is to be measured as much by the sheer number of ideas it throws up
directly or indirectly as by the 'correctness' of the
ideas put forward.   The foregoing should not be seen as a
digression, or material which might more appropriately
have been placed at the head of Chapter two.   It needs to
be said here because the corollary of it is that the
statement of the general democratic principles, which is
the subject of this chapter, will be of lesser importance.
In the context of this essay, therefore, relatively little
attempt will be made to compare in detail even major
writers on democratic theory like Rawls, Dworkin and
Ackerman, though from time to time signposts will be
erected, linking points made here to their influential
work in this field.

Let me turn then to the general principles and basic
assumptions underlying democracy.   I take as my starting
point the normal person, in particular the normal person
as a chooser. (1)   People all over the world all the
time, make choices.   They decide what to have for lunch,
to take baths, to curl their hair, when to irrigate their
crops.   The common-sense presumption is that the onus is
on anyone who wants to interfere with another's choices to
justify the interference.   The interference may be justifiable (the chooser is insane, an infant risking her
safety, etc.), but it has to be justified.   This is the
barest statement of a principle of freedom which takes as
unproblematic for the moment the notion of what is involved in 'making choices'.

Even this bare statement of the principle will, however, make the most stringent demands on anyone wanting to

justify the exercise of political power.   Political
power, after all, may be exercised in such a way as to
coerce me into filling up forms, driving on a certain side
of the road, giving up part of my income, taking up a certain occupation, not publishing my thoughts, even killing
people.   If anyone ever thought that the way to avoid
this clash with the principle of freedom was to reject the
whole idea of political power, then this view has been
quashed by Nozick (1974, especially Part I).   Whatever
else Nozick has shown, he has surely demonstrated that if
states did not exist we would have to invent them - or
back into them by degrees at least.   If however one rejects the anarchistic alternative and accepts that it is
in any person's interest that there be some political
power, some state apparatus, can any guidelines be established as to the morally permissible form of such a state?
Anyone tempted, in an unthinking way, to claim that a
democracy like the United Kingdom or the United States
would constitute such a morally permissible state, might
do well to reflect that according to Habermas (1976) these
countries, as advanced capitalist states, are held to be
experiencing a 'legitimation crisis'.   They are not then
unproblematically acceptable.   It may be that the demands
for justifications for their principles and practices can
be met, but such justifications have to be produced.   And
if they do not stand up, the question arises again of the
form political power would have to take to be acceptable.

If we lived in a radically different world, the form a
political state might take might be rather more obvious.
In a world where a minority of the population were normal
people, moderately rational, moderately benevolent, not
conspicuously lacking in strength of will, (2) and the
rest were feeble creatures, irrational, weak in understanding, weak in will power and with strong tendencies
towards the psychopathic, there would be grounds for maintaining that the political state should take a paternalistic form.   A benevolent despotism with the normal minority taking care of the interests of the weak minded majority, with careful and impartial benevolence, might well
be the most justifiable political arrangement.   Our
world, however, is not like that.   Overwhelmingly we are
all normal people.   And there are no super-people around,
constant in wisdom, rationality and strength of will, who
might have a claim to exercise power over us.   I say
'might have a claim' because the case has not actually
been made that if these super-people did exist, they would
be justified in virtue of the fact of their superior
wisdom, rationality, etc. in interfering with the plans,

intentions, purposes of us normal people.   If superior
intelligences from another planet arrived, would they be
justified - just like that - in taking over our political
affairs, national governments, the United Nations, etc.,
reorganizing them and running things for us?   Do we not
have to be shown to be incapable of conducting our own
lives in some way (i.e., very weak in understanding, etc.)
for such interference to be justified?   Will it do to
argue simply that the super-people will do it better?
What could 'do it better' mean here?   If it means help us
realize ends we already have in view more efficiently,
this is to supply advice and does not amount to 'running
things for us'.   If it means direct us towards 'better
ends', who is to say that they are better for us if we do
not recognize them as such?

    This fanciful example brings us back to our normal
world in which there are no super-intelligences, anyway,
so that even if such beings might have a claim to run our
political affairs for us, they are not available to do so.
As things are no one has a better claim to exercise political power over the rest of us, on grounds of superior
insight into the ends of life, for us individually and
collectively.   Therefore the only way to dispose of political power in a morally acceptable way is to allow each
individual access to an equal share in the exercise, or
control, of power.   This, I take it, is the basic case
for democracy.   When it is claimed that democracy rests
on the twin principles of freedom and justice, this is
what is enshrined in this basic formulation: each person
must have access to an equal share in the exercise, or
control of power, so that no conception of the good life
is arbitrarily imposed on anyone, and no one is subject to
arbitrary interference.   In formulating the case for
democracy in this way I am taking the view that the appropriate stance towards democracy is not to see it, for
instance, as a splendid way of encouraging the development
of certain sorts of admirable people, perhaps co-operative
or fraternal people.   One should rather see it negative-
ly, as the most morally acceptable form of government
available to protect individuals from the abuse of power
by an individual, a minority, or even a majority.   Democratic governments will also concern themselves with the
impartial promotion of the well-being of their citizens
but, after all, a benevolent despot might do this.   What
is uniquely characteristic of democracy is the demand that
the individual must share equally in the exercise, or control, of power, a demand which recognizes that no individual or group should have the power to impose preferences

for a certain style of life on others.   This conception
rests in turn on three basic assumptions which should be
made explicit at this point.

THREE BASIC ASSUMPTIONS

The first, most important and most basic assumption is
that there are no moral experts on the good life for individuals in detail.   In the long history of ethical
theory, despite continual attempts, no one has even
managed to demonstrate conclusively that broad styles of
life are to be preferred over other styles, for instance,
the active over the contemplative life or vice versa, the
life of the enthusiastic specialist over the urbane all-
rounder or vice versa and so on. (3)   The only authority
on the good life is therefore the individual himself or
herself who has had the chance to reflect on possible
lives.   The considered, reflective choice of such an
individual after he or she has been able to assess the
possibilities is not corrigible by any moral experts.   A
democratic government cannot therefore pursue policies
which endorse one conception of the good life as intrin-
sically superior to others.   This is an assumption held
by most liberal democratic theorists, like for instance
Dworkin (1978b) and Ackerman (1980).   Indeed Dworkin sees
this assumption as one of the constitutive elements of the
liberal position.   Interestingly it is also an assumption
which has a close parallel in a similar one made by Marx
and also contemporary Marxists, like for instance C.B.
Macpherson (1977).   They are not prepared to specify the
form of the good life for individuals in the future Communist society, because as they see it it is for the future
individuals to choose how best to fulfil their natures.
Since human interests and needs evolve historically, it is
only possible to be agnostic about the choices future
individuals in a changed social context might make.   This
theoretical similarity in one important aspect of Marxist
and liberal theory, namely their agnostic views on the
good for man, suggests that in so far as their practice in
each case realized their theory there would be a real possibility for some reconciliation between Marxist and
liberal political systems.

So unless and until some breakthrough is achieved in
the determination of the good life for individuals by
experts (if that is indeed a conceivable project and I am
not sure that it is) the democratic assumption that the
government and other institutions in the society shall

not, either directly or indirectly, favour one conception
of the good life over another must remain unchallenged.

Secondly this agnosticism about the good life gives
firm guidelines on a number of further assumptions which a
government must make and embody in its policies if it is
concretely to realize this stance.   These assumptions -
about particular goods which a government should guarantee
to its citizens - are commonplace among democratic theorists.   Perhaps more remarkably, there is considerable
agreement on the list of such goods.   The basic idea is
that certain goods and rights are necessary means to the
realization of a wide number of different conceptions of
the good life.   The kinds of goods I have in mind are
opportunities and wealth and the traditional civil rights:
freedom of thought and conscience and the rule of law, and
the right to participate in the exercise, or control of
power.   This bare and abstract list, which closely
follows Rawls's list of 'primary goods', is unlikely to be
controversial (Rawls, 1972, section 15).   What is more
likely to be so are the kinds of institutions and practices which will be suggested in Chapter two as ways of
realizing policies which will secure these goods to
people.   To cite a case particularly relevant to this
essay, Rawls includes in his list of primary goods 'opportunities and powers' but does not explore the kind of
institutional machinery which might secure 'opportunities'
to people.   A fundamental piece of such machinery, it
seems to me, must be education, but Rawls is not alone
amongst contemporary political theorists in not tracing
the implications of his political theory for a theory of
education.   As Dworkin (1978a) has said:

> It does seem to me that liberalism is rather weak at
> this point and needs a theory of education and a theory
> of culture-support that it does not have.   That, I
> think is part of the answer to the question: 'Where
> must political theory go?'

Some suggestions for machinery necessary to secure these
primary goods to citizens will be made in Chapter two,
particularly in respect of the goods - e.g. opportunities,
freedom of thought and conscience, participation in the
exercise, or control, of political power - which are relevant to the topic of this essay.

Third, come assumptions about the nature of the persons
who inhabit the community in question.   These assumptions
fall into two sets.   The first set comprises those

capacities and abilities which it may be supposed all
normal human beings possess by nature and to which H.L.A.
Hart has drawn attention (Hart, 1961, pp. 189-95).   I am
thinking of things like limited understanding and strength
of will, which make it possible, for instance, for our
behaviour to be rule-guided.   Into the same category
would come our capacity for altruism, the fact that we are
neither undeterrable devils nor angels.   It is these
attributes which make any government both possible and
necessary.

The second set of assumptions relate to the attributes
of democratic citizens in particular.   A great deal has
been written on the 'democratic character' presupposed by
the democratic state.   It is into this tradition, I
think, that Rawls's work on his suggested primary good of
'self-esteem' fits.   There is considerable work to be
done in examining these accounts of the democratic character and sifting out what is necessary for citizens in a
democratic state, what is permissible and what is unnecessary, if not directly in conflict with democratic ideals.
That is not a job to be attempted here.   I will simply
restrict myself to what I want to claim are some necessary
attributes of the democratic citizen which the community
will want to have developed in its members.

Given the fundamental agnosticism on the good life
which is a basic assumption the community will have to see
that citizens develop who are capable of appreciating
ideals of life and reflectively considering them as possible options for themselves (a).   In other words they
will need to be able to make choices.   They will need as
well of course the kind of institutions which permit and
enrich choices, but do not enforce them (cf. Chapter two).
Going along with these attributes they will need an
absence of certain character-traits like servility and a
desire to follow the crowd.   They will also need confidence and courage to adopt unfashionable ways themselves
if they consider these to be right and/or to defend others
who wish to do so.   This second point leads us beyond the
self regarding attributes noted under (a), to (b), the un-
prejudiced tolerance of others and their chosen ways of
life which the democratic citizen will need to manifest.
This is the point perhaps at which to emphasize that this
is not an individualistic conception of democracy in the
sense that its rationale is the autonomous citizen standing up for his/her rights in the face of state power, or
the power of institutions or other individuals.   Since,
as we have seen, the state (or any other institution) has

no reason to show any preference towards any conception of
the good life rather than any other, if citizens find a
way of life preferred or downgraded by the state they
will, quite literally, have no reason to endorse this and
every reason to oppose it and attempt to get the state of
affairs redressed.   If by some design, or even lucky
chance, my chosen way of life happens to be favoured by
state policies, given the assumptions of agnosticism about
the good life which we are working with, I have no reason,
it would be irrational of me, not to oppose this.   Agnosticism about the good life brings with it reasons for justice and tolerance towards others' chosen ways of life and
no reason for me to accept a policy which gives mine or
anyone else's a privileged place.

The attributes noted under (a) and (b) are not exhaustive even of the main attributes of the democratic citizen
but they are an attempt to make a start in this area,
which is supplemented in Chapter two. (4)   The whole
account has far-reaching implications for the conduct of
education in its widest sense.

Before discussing the applications of the basic democratic principle to actual historical societies in Chapter
two let me make four general points about the democratic
exercise, or control, of power in any society.

PARTICIPATORY DEMOCRACY

The first is that if the basic principle is equality in
the exercise, or control, of power, then the presumption
always must be for what has come to be called a participatory democracy.   As things stand in the literature of
democratic theory at the moment the reader gets the
impression that participatory democracy is only one of a
number of possible forms that democracy can take.   There
is supposedly some core of democratic values which all
forms of it share but for those holding some particular
constellation of values, which either give special emphasis to something in the core or which tack on additional
values - those, for instance, of markedly egalitarian
leanings or those anxious to promote the ideal of the
active citizen - there is the option of participatory
democracy.   It is held that those wanting to give this
particular twist to democracy must produce arguments to
justify their version.   It is not like this however.   In
fact the case is exactly reversed.   The presumption is
for participatory democracy, i.e. equality in the exercise

of power, and it is departures from this which have to be
·justified.   That is why until this point I have talked
about equality in the exercise, or control of power,
because in those cases where equality in the exercise of
power would either be totally impracticable or would
defeat or seriously damage the realization of justice,
freedom or other democratic values, it will be necessary
to move to equality in the control of power, the second
best situation.   Needless to say, the cases for impracti-
cability or damage to democratic values will need to be
strong ones, if they are to defeat the presumption in
favour of equality in the exercise of power.   As we have
seen, this presumption for the democratic exercise of
power, i.e. for a participatory democracy, rests on the
basic principle of justice as impartiality and thus is not
lightly defeated and cast aside.   It is worth emphasizing
this point because some of the cases which have been made
for participatory democracy (neatly summarized by Amy
Gutmann in Liberal Equality (Gutmann, 1980, pp. 178-83))
rest on empirical assumptions about, for instance, human
motivation or the best way of gathering information about
the consequences of policies.   Clearly if these proved to
be false those cases for participatory democracy would go
with them.   By contrast the present case for participatory democracy rests on the fundamental moral presumption
of the equality of all normal human beings as choosers.
This case will not be defeated by the discovery of new
empirical facts.   The citing of examples of human beings
who are not normal in this respect (e.g. who are perhaps
brain damaged) is irrelevant to this presumption since,
whatever provision should be made for them within the
democratic state, they will necessarily be excluded from
the exercise or control of power since this pre-eminently
involves choice.

The case for participatory democracy is then a strong
one and it poses a challenge to three current assumptions
of industrialized, capitalist democracies.

(i)   The first is the assumption that democracy is to be
seen as a certain method for arriving at political decisions.   As Schumpeter, still perhaps the most well-known
exponent of this view, puts it, the democratic method is
'that institutional arrangement for arriving at political
decisions in which individuals acquire the power to decide
by means of a competitive struggle for the people's vote'
(Schumpeter, 1976, p. 269).   On this view what is characteristic of democracy is a competition for leadership.
There is no question of the people participating in the

exercise of power by participating in decision-making at
any level, because Schumpeter holds 'the electoral mass is
incapable of action other than a stampede' (Schumpeter,
1976, p. 283).   The only role for citizens is to vote
when required and so keep the leadership competition
going.

What is curious about this conception of democracy is
that it is arrived at by arguing from an alleged fact
about the political interests and abilities of citizens in
particular societies to the value judgment that therefore
such poor creatures should have a certain kind of arrangement for making political decisions.   This is generally
characteristic of the so-called elite theorists of democracy whose positions Carole Pateman has documented in considerable detail (Pateman, 1970, Chapter 1).   As I have
argued, this procedure must be reversed.   One must start
from the presumption of equality in the exercise of power
and then see if a case might be made out which can defeat
it.   All well and good, an objector might claim at this
point, but this is simply a quibble, for when the presumption in favour of equality in the exercise of power is
made, it can be defeated by referring to the sorts of
facts which Schumpeter and later theorists cite.   Low
turn-out rates at local and national elections, little
interest even in participating in local community affairs,
the low-level, personality-oriented presentation of politics in the media and in political advertising campaigns
indicate both a lack of interest in politics on the part
of large parts of the population and also an inability to
grasp the intricacies of political argument.   These
points do not defeat the case, however.   To take first
the media point.   From the current policies of the media
in presenting political affairs, as well as from the inane
slogans and campaigns dreamed up by advertising companies
for political parties, we can deduce nothing about what
people might, or might not, be able to understand or take
an interest in where political matters are concerned.   In
our present societies we have strong grounds for thinking
that the media and the parties are not, even half of the
time, making an all-out effort to raise the political consciousness of the population, with the idea of encouraging
an interest in, and a vigorous examination and critique of
our society's dominant institutions and their policies and
practices.   We cannot judge the level of political understanding that might be achieved, therefore, by the current
presentation of political affairs by the media and the
party propaganda machines.   Before we could get any pur-
chase on that problem we would at least need to have had

an opportunity to see the kind of political education
policies outlined in Chapter three in action.

The points I want to make about participation rates are
not unconnected with these points about the media.   There
is first a formal similarity between the two cases.   Just
as in the media case, we can respond to the data on low
participation rates, e.g. low electoral turn-outs, etc. by
saying that since these data were collected in the kind of
democracies Schumpeter and the elite theorists are describing we cannot draw any firm conclusions about what
levels of participation one might expect in a participatory democracy.   What seems clear from various studies
(Verba and Nie, 1972) is that people tend to participate
politically if they believe that their participation will
significantly affect the outcome.   In contemporary democracies many people judge realistically that they literally
have better things to do than vote.   Secondly, there are
claimed to be cross-cultural correlations between levels
of participation and levels of education and socioeconomic
status (Verba, Nie and Kim, 1971).   The higher the socioeconomic status and level of education of a person the
more likely she is to participate.   These correlations
tend to suggest that one's knowledge of political matters,
wealth, concomitant style of life and amount and timing of
leisure are most probably connected with one's willingness
and ability to participate in political affairs.

As things stand at the moment, therefore, it would be a
wildly injudicious person who would judge on the basis of
the studies of political participation rates and the presentation of political matters in the media that the presumption in favour of equality in the exercise of power
has been defeated.   Indeed it would be distinctly odd if
investigations did find high levels of political participation in contemporary capitalist elite democracies,
because, as Habermas points out, the public realm of such
societies with its periodic plebiscites is 'structurally
depoliticized.'   Essential to the maintenance of the
system is 'civil privatism' - 'political abstinence combined with an orientation to career, leisure and consump-
tion' (Habermas, 1976, p. 37).   As Habermas argues later,
efforts at participation and initiatives by citizens
threaten the depoliticized realm.

Participatory democracy withstands, then, the first
challenge from the elite theorists and their data on political apathy and ignorance.   The case against participatory democracy on those grounds is simply not proven.

There remain, of course, a number of questions about the
kind(s) of machinery appropriate to realize a participatory democracy in contemporary societies.   These will be
tackled in Chapter two.

(ii)   The first challenge to participatory democracy came
from a position which wanted to restrict the exercise of
political power to an elite.   This was shown to be an
arbitrary and indefensible restriction.   The second challenge involves a claim to restrict the area of political
power itself, with the parallel claim that other areas in
which power is exercised are not political and must not be
subject to political 'interference'.   Thus advocates of
minimal government argue that the organization of industry
and commerce must not be interfered with for 'political'
reasons, private education must similarly not be queried
for purely 'political' reasons and so on.   However, like
Ackerman, I would want to say: 'While proposals for "minimal" government differ in detail, I take their essence to
be a refusal to permit the state to question the overall
distribution of power in society' (Ackerman, 1980, p. 253).
Participatory democracy, however, rests on quite the opposite presumption, namely that any exercise of power should
be shared equally between all those involved, unless this
can be shown, as I said above, to be either impracticable
or damaging to the realization of democratic values in
other ways.

   The presumption is therefore that in all the institutions of any society - all work-places, schools, hospitals,
libraries, sports centres, theatres, etc. - power will be
exercised democratically or subject to democratic control.
Needless to say the division between exercise and control
of power will be different for different institutions and
the kind of machinery appropriate will also vary.   In
Chapter two the kind of machinery suitable in the work-
place will be discussed.   In Chapters three, four and
five questions of the exercise and control of power in the
conduct of education in some of its formal and informal
aspects will be examined.

(iii)   These last points about the extent of the participatory democracy may well provoke a general objection to
what might be termed the 'politicizing' of virtually the
whole of a person's life.   Some people, it might be
argued, are not interested in politics: they simply want
to do an honest day's work, get treatment in hospitals
when they need it, and enjoy their leisure and so on.
They do not want to be involved in running their factory,

the hospital where they go for treatment, their local
sports centre, etc.   Have such people (perhaps most of
us?) a duty to participate in the exercise or control of
power in these various institutions?

There are three main points to be made here.

First, if, as I have argued, there are good grounds,
deriving ultimately from the principle of justice, for
thinking that power in any institution should be subject
to democratic exercise or control, then the fact of
people's apathy or even hostility to what they might see
as an illegitimate extension of the realm of the political, cannot, just like that, count as an argument against
it.   It will rather be a matter of getting people to
appreciate, through political education, that they have
both moral rights and, more pertinently here, moral duties
in an area where it may not have occurred to them that the
they did, or where they are reluctant to acknowledge them.

To anticipate, secondly, the discussion in Chapter two,
the exercise and control of power will not take the same
form in all institutions.   The kind of machinery required
in an institution which has a massive capacity to affect
its members and/or the community's interests will be very
different from that required to regulate the lesser power
available to be wielded at, say, the local sports centre.
It would be quite misleading, therefore, to imagine every
citizen overwhelmed by meetings to be attended, and committee papers to be read for every institution with which
she has any connection.   In this respect participatory
democracy has had a bad press: an image of endless discussion in smoke-filled rooms has served as a substitute
for the concrete examination of the machinery which might
be involved.   When that has been done the bureaucratic
burden on individual citizens may not seem so oppressive.

The burdensomeness of burdens, thirdly, is relative.
To someone who, say, wants to devote all her energies to a
work on ethical theory, even the slightest involvement in
the running of her work-place, local residents' associa-
tion or whatever will appear as a monstrous encroachment.
What is the position of such a citizen?   This, it seems
to me, is the familiar case of a person faced by a clash
between two prima facie moral duties.   On any particular
occasion, or at any particular period of time, it must be
a matter for individual moral persons to decide which of
their duties takes precedence over others with competing
claims on their time and energies.   Clearly any particular

decision one makes will be made in the light of familiar
moral considerations and will be potentially criticizable
in familiar ways as, e.g. thoughtless, selfish, etc.   I
am not, however, concerned with the particular way in
which any individual might make her decision on any particular occasion.   I want rather to point out that what a
citizen cannot do, as a rational moral agent, is to
decide, in general, that moral concern stops on the other
side of the factory gates, the sports centre threshold,
etc.   As a rational moral person she has to remain at
least minimally politically aware in respect of the institutions in society with which she is involved, ready to
judge, for instance, that her duties at the work-place at
the moment take precedence over other moral duties, for
the possibility that they might cannot be ruled out in
advance.   People cannot decide, once and for all, that
they will simply do an 'honest day's work' and let others
get on with the politics, because to do so would be to run
the risk of, e.g. not having done what one might to prevent some serious injustice.

In general, then, there is a duty to participate in the
exercise, or control, of power in relevant institutions.
It is not an absolute one, because the citizen must be
free to decide on any particular occasion that it is overridden by another more pressing one, but it is a prima
facie duty.

POWER

In this chapter I have made repeated references to the
exercise, or control, of power.   This notion is a central
one in this essay and I need now to lay bare what I am
understanding by it.   This is important because, as we
shall see, different conceptions of power have different
implications for the moral acceptability of different political arrangements and their associated educational
arrangements.

In this section I shall be following closely Steven
Lukes's account of different conceptions of power in
Power: a Radical View.   In that book Lukes is concerned
not with 'power to' - i.e. a capacity or ability - but
with 'power over' - i.e. a relationship.   Lukes discusses
three views of power which he sees as alternative inter-
pretations of one and the same underlying concept of
power.   According to the underlying concept, A exercises
power over B when A affects B in a manner contrary to B's

interests.   In so far as one person affects another significantly without there being a conflict of interests,
that is not an instance of one person exercising power
over another but something else - for instance some form
of influence.

The first interpretation which Lukes discusses is that
of the American 'pluralists', notably R.A. Dahl.   This
focuses on the making of decisions on issues over which
there is a conflict of interests embodied in different
policy preferences.   A classic example of an exercise of
power on this view would be a clash between a government
and a trade union, where each favours a different policy
and where one side is induced by some threat of sanctions
on the part of the other to give up its chosen policy.
This is all right as far as it goes but it does not manage
to capture even all major instances of the exercise of
power in the real world.

The second view, represented by the work of Bachrach
and Baratz, is something of a corrective to the first in
that they are interested not only in decision-making but
also in nondecision-making.   A decision is 'a choice
among alternative modes of action' (Bachrach and Baratz,
1970, p. 39);   a nondecision is a 'decision that results
in suppression or thwarting of a latent or manifest challenge to the values or interests of the decision-maker'
(Bachrach and Baratz, 1970, p. 44).   Thus, nondecision-
making is

> a means by which demands for change in the existing
> allocation of benefits and privileges in the community
> can be suffocated before they are even voiced;   or kept
> covert;   or killed before they gain access to the rele-
> vant decision-making arenas;   or, failing all these
> things, maimed or destroyed in the decision-implement-
> ing stage of the policy process (Bachrach and Baratz,
> 1970, p. 44).

For Bachrach and Baratz therefore it is important to identify potential issues which nondecision-making prevents
from being actual.   In taking this stand they are of
course firmly rejecting Dahl's view that 'a political
issue can hardly be said to exist unless and until it com-
mands the attention of a significant segment of the political stratum' (Dahl, 1961, p. 92), which leaves them with
the problem of identifying key political issues.   This
they resolve by regarding a key issue as 'one that involves a genuine challenge to the resources of power or

authority of those who currently dominate the process by
which policy outputs in the system are determined', that
is, 'a demand for enduring transformation in both the
manner in which values are allocated in the polity ... and
the value allocation itself' (Bachrach and Baratz, 1970,
pp. 47-8).   Bachrach and Baratz mark an advance on the
first view in focusing on nondecision-making as well as
decision-making, but like the holders of the first view
they still want to stress the importance of actual observable conflict in revealing exercises of power in nondecision-making.   They say 'if there is no conflict overt or
covert, the presumption must be that there is consensus on
the prevailing allocation of values, in which case nondecision-making is impossible' (Bachrach and Baratz, 1970,
p. 49).   The conflict they consider necessary is that
between the interests of those engaged in nondecision-
making and the interests of those they exclude from a
hearing within the political system.   The latter interests will, they claim, be 'observable in their aborted
form to the investigator' (Bachrach and Baratz, 1970, p.
49).   The second view, then, allows for consideration of
the ways in which decisions are prevented from being taken
on potential issues over which there is an observable conflict of interests, seen as embodied in express policy
preferences and sub-political grievances.

The second view, although an improvement on the first
in incorporating into the analysis of power relations the
question of the control over the agenda of politics and
the ways in which potential issues are kept out of the
political process, still fails to pick up important instances of the exercise of power.   According to Lukes it
is inadequate in three ways.   First, in focusing on decisions and assimilating all cases of exclusion of potential
issues from the political agenda to decisions to suppress
issues,etc., it gives only a partial picture of the way in
which groups and institutions succeed in excluding potential issues.   In fact 'the power to control the agenda of
politics and exclude potential issues cannot be adequately
analysed unless it is seen as a function of collective
forces and social arrangements' (Lukes, 1974, p. 22).   In
Schattschneider's well-known phrase 'the mobilisation of
bias' results from the form of the organization, from the
socially structured and culturally patterned practices of
institutions, which may be manifested by individuals' in-
action.   Organizations are of course made up of individuals, but the power they exercise cannot simply be accoun-
ted for in terms of individuals' decisions.   We shall see
the importance of this interpretation of power when we

come in due course to look in Chapter three at the organization of educational institutions.

In assuming secondly that where there is no observable
conflict, even in some abortive form, there is no exercise
of power, Bachrach and Baratz made a big mistake with far-
reaching implications.   Clearly power can be exercised in
the absence of conflict and this is so in perhaps the most
successful exercises of power.   A may exercise power over
B by getting B to do what B does not want to do but he
also exercises power over B by controlling, shaping and
determining B's very wants, so that B comes to want exactly what A wants him to want.   The most secure governing
elites, for instance, are those in a situation where the
governed accept both the elite and their own subordinate
role as the legitimate order, so that secret police and
the accompanying paraphernalia of state coercion are unnecessary.   Any account of power must allow for the fact
that the most successful forms of power do not involve
conflict but prevent its ever arising.

The third mistake is closely connected with the second.
It is the assumption that if people feel no grievances,
they they have no interests which are harmed by the use of
power.   Again, however, the supreme exercise of power
will prevent people from having grievances by shaping
their desires, perceptions of the world and their place in
it.   To assume that the absence of grievances means that
there is genuine consensus on values and the allocation of
resources is to ignore the possibility that consensus can
be manipulated.

The third view of power, developed by Lukes, builds on
and considerably extends, the second view.   It allows for
the many ways in which potential issues are kept out of
politics, whether by individuals' decision or, perhaps
more likely, by the very organization of politics and
institutional practices.   It also allows that this may
occur in the absence of any observable conflict, which may
have been successfully averted.   There is however always
a potential conflict present, but one which may never be
realized, between the interests of those exercising power
and the 'real interests' of those they exclude.

There are three points to be made about Lukes's interpretation of the concept of power which together elaborate
it and raise, and answer, obvious objections.

(i) In the first place Lukes rejects an analysis of power

which takes people and their wants as they are as a matter
of fact.   Wants, as I have suggested above, can be manipulated and many exercises of power consist in exactly
this.   What A is doing may not be contrary to B's wants,
but it may be an exercise of power, or rest on a previous
exercise of power, for all that.   Lukes therefore intro-
duces the notion of 'real interests'.   A exercises power
over B when he affects B contrary to B's real interests,
even if not contrary to his wants.   B's 'real interests'
are what he would want or prefer were he in a position to
make a choice, i.e. were he in a position to be autonomous.   Lukes points out that this claim needs to be supported by 'a substantial discussion of the nature of, and
conditions for, autonomy' and refers to the beginnings of
such a discussion in his Individualism (1973).   This
present essay, although not offering a sustained discus
sion of autonomy, attempts to outline some aspects of the
kind of social structure required to permit people, as far
as possible, to live autonomous lives (Chapter two) as
well as to sketch some of the necessary educational conditions for the development of autonomy (Chapters three,
four and five).   I would hope that these discussions
would lend support to the kind of distinction Lukes wants
to draw between wants and 'real interests' because some
such distinction is vital to any analysis of power.

(ii)   However, if in his analysis of power Lukes wants to
say that to exercise power is to affect a person contrary
to his interests, does this mean that power cannot be
exercised by A over B in B's real interests?   If so, this
would seem to rule out classic cases of the exercise of
power, for instance, snatching the knife away from the
drunkard, pulling the unwary person back from the rotten
bridge, preventing the child from drinking weedkiller.
Lukes of course recognizes such cases (Lukes, 1974, p. 33)
and sees them as instances of 'short-term power', where
there is an observable conflict of 'subjective interests'.
However if, and when, B recognizes his 'real interests'
(in all the above three straightforward cases - in staying
alive) the conflict ends and with it the power relationship.   The safeguard against paternalism is that the
identification of B's real interests is not up to A but up
to B when he is able to exercise autonomous choice.

(iii)   The real problem for Lukes, though, arises in the
application of this analysis to the real world.   How does
one identify exercises of power in those important cases
where A does nothing and there is no observable conflict
with B?   How does one study a non-event?   It is precisely

the difficulty of identifying empirically such exercises
of power that has led so many investigators, Lukes claims,
to concentrate on those exercises of power in which there
is actual observable conflict.   He argues, however, that
in the non-event cases, too, it is possible to set up
empirically supportable and refutable hypotheses.   It is
not easy but it is, in principle, possible.   One needs
(a) to justify the expectation that B would have thought
or acted differently and (b) to specify the means by which
A has prevented, or else acted in a manner sufficient to
prevent, B from doing so.

Lukes mentions one empirical study in which this was
done, a study which asked why the issue of air pollution
was not raised as early or as effectively in some American
cities as in others (Crenson, 1971).   To quote Lukes:

> Crenson's analysis is impressive because it fulfills
> the double requirement mentioned above: there is good
> reason to expect that, other things being equal, people
> would rather not be poisoned (assuming in particular,
> that pollution control does not necessarily mean unem-
> ployment) - and even where they may not even articulate
> this preference;   and hard evidence is given of the
> ways in which institutions, specifically U.S. Steel,
> largely through inaction, prevented the citizen's
> interests in not being poisoned from being acted on
> (though other factors, institutional and ideological,
> would need to enter a fuller explanation).   Thus both
> the relevant counter factual and the identification of
> a power mechanism are justified (Lukes, 1974, p. 45).

Lukes see the difficulties, then, of identifying instances
of the suppression of latent conflicts within a society
but refuses to see these as overwhelming.

The exercise of power by a person or a group or an institution is always objectionable and always to be regretted.
It always involves affecting a person in a manner contrary
to his/her interests.   It would clearly be ideal if power
relationships could be completely eliminated from human
life.   This is however impossible.   Even without the
complication of what Lukes terms 'short-term power' being
exercised over babies and children, the absence of a total
consensus on values and the allocation of resources
amongst adult human beings means that sometimes some
people will be affected by institutions and policies in a
way contrary to their (or some of their) interests.

Power relationships cannot be eliminated from human life but in different social set-ups they can be present to a greater or lesser degree. The claim of this essay is that in a democracy exercises of power are fewer than in other political systems.

I make this claim basically on two grounds.

(i) In a democracy, which is of course a participatory democracy, there will be considerably more control by individuals themselves over matters in which they have interests. If individuals participate in decision-making in political arenas, in their work-places, sports centres, schools, hospitals, etc., or have some control over the decision-makers, there is less likelihood of their interests being simply ignored, or overruled because they are in some sense misperceived. This is of course John Stuart Mill's argument for people being 'able, and habitually disposed, to stand up for their [rights and interests]' (Mill, 1910, p. 208) so that these interests are not overlooked or seen with very different eyes by a ruling elite, which is not necessarily concerned knowingly and deliberately to sacrifice their interests. If I have some control over the arrangements at my work-place there is more chance of arrangements being in line with my interests than if my foreman, manager or boss makes them without reference to me and perhaps contrary to my interests, thus, even if unwittingly, exercising power over me.

This claim may well be questioned, however. It might be argued that individuals will be subject to exercises of power just as much in a democracy as in any other system. They will have, after all, to participate even if this seems to them to be contrary to their interests. Also since participation will be all-pervasive, the pressures on them to be involved will be hard to escape. It may indeed be easier to escape the tyrannical rule of a totalitarian state apparatus by lying low and, when necessary, confusing the bureaucracy. To make this kind of objection is, however, to ignore the points made earlier about the 'duty to participate' (see above p. 17f). Without repeating those in detail I should nevertheless link two of them with the analysis of power advanced here. In the first place convinced democrats will not see their participation in the exercise of power in general as against their interests, since, on the account presented here, they will have strong interests in the equal promotion of their own and others' capacity to make autonomous choices. [Those who take a very different view in general of their

interests, who, say, would see it as in their interests to
have their lives directed entirely by some spiritual
being, could obviously not be citizens of a democratic
society in the sense outlined here and would perhaps hive
themselves off to establish some form of theocracy.]
Secondly, in so far as the democratic citizen's interest
in autonomy clashes with other interests, or in so far as
the interest in the exercise of autonomy in one sphere
clashes with its exercise in another, in a particular case
the individual is clearly free to make her own choice as
to where her duty lies (cf. the case of the writer of the
Ethics book and the clash of duties). This kind of objection - that people will be forced, contrary to their
interests, to participate - cannot be made to support the
case that a democracy will exercise as much if not more
power than other political systems over its citizens.

(ii) The second ground for claiming that there will be
fewer exercises of power is that the manipulation and
shaping of people's wants, contrary to their interests,
will be outlawed. The subtleties of the processes which
may be at work in moulding people's wants are such that
the total elimination of such moulding is probably impossible. Nevertheless education in understanding the
phenomenon of the exercise of power, will alert people to
the many and subtle ways in which it may be manifested so
that they will be enabled to combat it in both personal
and institutional ways. In such a society, where people
are intent on identifying and nullifying such manipulative
exercises of power and building institutional bulwarks
against them - watchdog committees, Ombudspersons, judicial reviews, etc. etc. - other things being equal, there
must be fewer exercises of power than in a society where,
say, an elite ruling group is bent on keeping the people
happy. Of course an education which aims, in part, to
get people to understand the complexities and mechanisms
of power may not necessarily lead every moral agent to
become a democrat. I am not concerned with the person
who puts herself outside the moral framework altogether
and decides to seek as much power over others as possible
but with the moral person who appreciates the connection
between the exercise of power and interests and realizes
that if she has the kind of interests which power-wielders
cannot attack, she is effectively out of their range.
She has the perfect defence against them and needs no
institutional shields. In the extreme case I am thinking
of the kind of religious mystic, who has (literally) no
interest in the world, and simply desires to enter the
next world as soon as possible. Clearly few exercises of

power are going to affect her.   However, as I said above,
I am not concerned in this essay to argue for appropriate
political arrangements for a person with a religious picture of the good life which either dominates over her
other interests, or constitutes her sole interest.
Otherwise, for most people with varying conceptions of the
good life, the institutions of democracy constitute the
best safeguard against arbitrary exercises of power.

In my general claim that in a democracy there will be
fewer exercises of power I am in agreement, I think, with
Carole Pateman in The Problem of Political Obligation.
The only difference between us is, if I have understood
her correctly, that she thinks there will be very, very
few exercises of power in a political society characterized by 'self-assumed political obligation'.   Pateman
takes this view, I think, because she sees power and
authority relationships as quite distinct.   She says:

> It is often assumed that the 'political' refers to
> power relationships.... A democratic transformation of
> the liberal democratic state can then appear to presage
> an end of the political itself.   However, ... the col-
> lective dimension of social life cannot disappear;
> rather the aim of democratic political change is, as
> far as possible, to transform power relationships into
> relationships of authority in which citizens collec-
> tively exercise political authority (Pateman, 1979,
> p. 175).

Pateman does not make clear exactly what she has in mind
in talking about the transformation of power relationships
into authority relationships.   I presume it is something
like the following.   Both power and authority are causal
notions.   In power situations A affects B in some way or
other contrary to B's interests.   This does not involve
consent on B's part.   In authority situations, A also
affects B in some way or other, possibly contrary to B's
interests, but here A has the right to do so and in the
kind of democratic society Pateman and I have in mind, A's
right to direct B's actions (etc.) is always exercised
with B's consent.   Pateman is thus making the following
distinction: in a democratic society the dictator's power
has been transformed into the collective exercise of political authority.   This latter, according to Pateman, is
wrongly construed as an exercise of power since it involves the consent of citizens.   Therefore there will be
fewer exercises of power because power has been transformed into authority.   Lukes would also probably accept

this, I think, since he wants to say that 'Consensual
authority, with no conflict of interests, is not, therefore, a form of power' (Lukes, 1974, p. 32).   Peters,
too, makes the same point.   'The concept of "authority"
is necessary to bring out the ways in which behaviour is
regulated without recourse to power' (Peters, 1967, p. 93).

I am left with a residual doubt however.   If we make
this sharp distinction between authority and power, and
furthermore if we talk about power relationships being
transformed into authority relationships in the democratic
society, we shall be tempted to overlook some possible
exercises of power in a democratic society through the
democratic machinery itself.   What I particularly have in
mind are the kind of conflicts which arise between majorities and minorities in a democratic society.   I am not
even assuming that these are permanent majorities and
minorities - though the problem is exacerbated if they
are.   Citizens have agreed, let us assume, to the practice of majority voting to decide certain issues.   Without anticipating the discussion in Chapter two, let us
imagine that one of these issues is the allocation of certain resources.   The particular case we might take is the
provision of some leisure facility in a small community. (5)   Money is available for either a swimming pool
or a theatre but not for both, and any division of resources will not be sufficient to finance either adequately.
People have to vote and it is agreed that they do so
according to their personal preference for one facility or
the other.   (There is no need to complicate matters at
this point by introducing Dworkin's distinction between
personal and external preferences.   See Chapter two, pp.
55-6.)   The result is, let us say, that a majority want
the swimming pool and a minority the theatre.   Let us
assume that the minority is not won over to the majority's
point of view.   Those in the minority would still prefer
the theatre, but since they assent in general to the democratic machinery and previously assented to this particular way of settling the policy decision, they decide to go
along with the majority vote.   In such cases Pateman
wants to say that 'a kind of unanimity results' (Pateman,
1979, p. 161).   Certainly this is one way of describing
the situation, if one focuses on the fact that both majority and minority are united in agreeing that the decision
to go ahead with the swimming pool should be implemented.
There is, however, another way of looking at the situation.   One can see it, to put matters simply, as a situation in which the majority has two interests satisfied and
the minority has one interest satisfied and one denied.

By that I mean that the majority's interest in taking the
decision within a democratic framework and according to
the agreed procedure of majority voting is satisfied; so
also is its interest in having a swimming pool.   The
minority's interest in taking the decision within a democratic framework, etc. is also similarly satisfied; but
its interest in having a theatre is not.   According to
the analysis of power with which we have been working,
therefore, a practice (majority voting) is affecting the
minority in a way contrary to one of its interests.
Viewed in one way, therefore, the minority is subject to
an exercise of power.   Whilst I agree that the situation
can be viewed differently as an example of 'a kind of
unanimity', if one focuses on the agreement over the
implementation of the decision, it seems to me important
also to see that it can be viewed, as one might say, as 'a
kind of exercise of power', if one focuses on the fact
that the voting procedure is affecting the minority contrary to its interests.   With a permanent minority the
situation is, of course, very much worse and aptly described by the phrase 'the tyranny of the majority'.

  Some people might want to resist this second way of
viewing the majority/minority case.   They might want to
rule out the possibility of 'permanent majorities' in a
self-managed democracy and to argue that policy decisions
would be taken with the good of the whole community in
mind and would not be contrary to individuals' interests.
However, without dealing with these points now so as not
to anticipate the discussion of Chapter two, I want to
suggest that even in a democracy there will be, on occasion, decisions of the kind described above and in so far
as that is the case the minority can be seen as in a power
situation.   Democrats must be aware of this way of viewing the situation and monitor the frequency of these
occurrences so as to counterbalance these exercises of
power as far as possible, since they are unlikely to be
completely eliminable.   It may be useful in some contexts
to talk of citizens in a democracy as exercising political
authority rather than power so as to highlight the difference between democratic societies and any form of tyranny,
namely that in a democracy there is consent to procedures
by means of which the wielding of power is shared, or controlled.   It is however dangerous to see the democratic
society as transformed from a power society into a consensual authority one, since this may produce an undue com-
placency and make us less alert to exercises of power embedded in political procedures.   Since there is a measure
of indeterminateness about the application of the concepts

of power and authority, (6) and since one's use of them is
going to be determined in part by the context, I have in
this essay preferred to describe democracy as the kind of
political arrangement where the exercise of power is
shared or controlled, according to certain agreed procedures.   This is because exercises of power harm people
and I have wanted to focus on the prevention and control
of this harm - by literally keeping it before our eyes on
the page - rather than on the procedures for controlling
it - which is what tends to happen if one talks of democracy in terms of consensual authority.

ECONOMIC POWER AND THE DISTRIBUTION OF WEALTH

I have stressed so far the basic equality of access to the
exercise, or control, of political power which must obtain
in a democracy.   That, however, must be matched by a
similarly egalitarian approach to the distribution of
income and wealth.   I want to make just two points about
this of a general sort because to pursue the issues raised
by it in detail would take me too far away from the main
educational themes of this essay.   There are two reasons,
which must apply in any democracy, for an egalitarian
approach to the distribution of wealth and income.   On
the one hand there is the basic egalitarian assumption
that any individual has as much right to an equal share in
the resources of his/her society as any other and any depar-
ture from this principle must be justified.   As far as a
citizen's basic welfare is concerned, therefore, each has
a right to a basic minimum to cover needs like food,
shelter, clothing, medical care, education and so on.
This is absolutely essential whatever conception of the
good life he/she may wish to realize.   It is essential if
he/she is even going to be able to raise and reflectively
consider that question.   At this point many readers will
no doubt query my use of the word 'essential' and feel
tempted to produce examples of people who lack these
things and nevertheless reflect on this question.   It is
not hard to think of struggling artists, desperately sick
people, people in concentration camps whose basic needs
are not met and who yet manage to reflect on the question
of the good life for man.   These kinds of examples cannot
be denied but on the one hand many of these people could
not realize their conceptions and, more importantly, one
can ask whether one should rest one's assumptions about
the basic needs of citizens in a democracy on these rather
exceptional individuals or on the 'normal citizen'.

The second reason for an egalitarian approach to the
distribution of income and wealth is that if equality of
access to political power is to be secured, it must not be
possible for an unequal distribution of economic power to
frustrate this.   This is a familiar point made by a great
number of writers in this area both classical and modern -
e.g. Rousseau, Rawls, Honderich - and nicely summed up in
this quotation from Dahl: 'if it could be quantified, I
suppose that Mr. Henry Luce has a thousand or ten thousand
times greater control over the alternatives scheduled for
debate and tentative decision at a national election than
I do' (Dahl, 1956, p. 72).   This kind of economic power
over the political agenda must be ruled out in a democracy.   This second reason for an egalitarian approach
does not absolutely rule out any differences in income and
wealth between citizens (since the presumption in favour
of equal treatment may be overridden; all may receive
equal consideration but different treatment may be justifiable), but it does limit the permitted range of income
differences.   If reasons can be produced, therefore, to
justify differences of income (e.g. perhaps motivational
reasons: the society needs to pay people more to go down
mines, clear out sewers, become doctors in geriatric hospitals), this would be possible provided that they were
not large.   It is not for me to say how large is 'large'
but presumably they should be as small as is compatible
with getting the job done.   Neither should it be assumed
that a democratic society would necessarily want to use
income differentials as incentives, the point being simply
that it would be compatible with the second reason for an
egalitarian approach to income and wealth for it to do so
within a limited range.

The twofold egalitarian approach which any democracy
must have towards the distribution of income and wealth
leaves open, to a considerable extent, how the division
between public and private property is to be made in any
particular society.   Once resources have been set aside
to cover the minimum welfare provision (which should not
incidentally be assumed to be a low minimum, as is usually
the case in contemporary societies), there is the question
of how the residue is to be distributed.   Several issues
arise at this point which may be resolved differently in
different democratic societies.   For instance, is the
residue to go largely to individuals or is it to go largely to public projects for communal use?   Clearly this
issue need not be settled in an either/or way; societies
may differ in how they tip the balance.   There is also
the question, raised already, of whether the residue

should be used in a modest income incentive scheme or not.
Democratic societies in different historical situations
may answer this question differently.

In any democratic society some institutions or organizations will have to be publicly owned by the community by
the nature of the function they perform.   Democratic communities cannot have private armies or private police
forces, but, those institutions aside, is it possible to
argue that in principle other resources and organizations
must be publicly owned?

I think that democrats should probably reject the question in the way that it is posed.   For as Dahl points
out, '"property" is a bundle of rights' (Dahl, 1970, p.
132) and these rights can be parcelled out in different
ways, as the rights of ownership over economic enterprises
are in Yugoslavia.   Once democrats view property in this
way, the conventional categories of public or private
ownership break down and it makes more sense to take the
bundle apart and consider an appropriate distribution of
the rights involved between central government, local communities, institutions themselves (industrial enterprises,
hospitals, libraries, banks, etc.) and individuals.
Therefore, after having hived off those institutions which
must be under direct state control, like the army and
police force, citizens would look at the bundle of rights
attached to any particular enterprise and see, in the
light of the basic principle about the equal sharing, or
control, of power, how these might be distributed.   Once
again, it is a matter of finding the appropriate machinery
to realize the basic principle.   There is room for considerable play here, with different societies dividing up
the bundle very differently, according to values they hold
which are permitted within the democratic framework,
though not required by it: some, for instance, may favour
communal projects over private ones and so on.

This discussion moves us on to Chapter two and its
examination of the general kinds of machinery which might
be appropriate to realize democracy in actual, historically situated societies.   It also anticipates the strategy
which will be employed later in tackling issues to do with
the control and organization of education.

Realising democratic principles: institutions and attitudes

2

Chapter one set out basic democratic principles and
assumptions.   Many people may find it possible to support
these broad principles and most of the associated assumptions, albeit from different (e.g. Utilitarian or Marxist)
standpoints.   These principles, however, have to be realized in particular historical societies and there is
likely to be much more controversy over how this should be
done.   For two reasons.   First, suggestions about institutions which might instantiate the principles are unlikely to command wide agreement.   Different people are
likely to conceive of alternative practices, policies,
etc., which seem to them much closer to the spirit of the
principles.   In the political systems with which we are
familiar, for instance, there are wide differences of
opinion on the relative fairness of such different voting
systems as first-past-the-post or proportional voting.
Second, the suggestions which follow are likely to encoun-
ter the objection that they are 'utopian' or at least
untried in practice, since the machinery suggested has not
been in operation anywhere in its complete form. (1)
Constructive brain-storming, however, as suggested in
Chapter one, can be useful in ironing out some of these
problems.   To some extent this process, as we shall see,
has begun already amongst theorists working in the participatory tradition of democracy.

PARTICIPATORY MACHINERY FOR POWER-SHARING

Before considering detailed pieces of machinery it is
useful to get a general picture of the kind of institutions and practices which would best realize equality in
the exercise, or control, of power in a whole society.
There is already a slender tradition of theorizing about

such machinery.   It is worth looking briefly at the work
of someone within this tradition whose basic principles
and assumptions, as also the problems which his suggestions for realizing those principles raise, are still the
concern of contemporary theorists.

In his Guild Socialism Restated G.D.H. Cole (1920) suggests machinery to realize very much the basic principles
set out in Chapter one.   He was anxious to secure equality of access to power, averse to any idea that it was
appropriate for leaders to lead the masses and opposed to
political centralism of any sort which might put the
levers of power in a few hands.   He said in 1917 that the
fundamental social evil requiring eradication is not poverty but slavery (Cole, 1917).   In this view he was obviously very close to Tawney, who had written in his Commonplace Book in 1912, 'The supreme evil of modern industrial society is not poverty.   It is the absence of,
liberty, i.e. of the opportunity for self-direction'
(quoted in Wright, 1979, p. 51, note 2).   It is clearly
liberty in this sense of self-direction which is at the
heart of Cole's suggestions at that time for the form of
work-place democracy called 'Guild Socialism'.   In 1918
he expresses similar sentiments in distinguishing his
views from those of Sidney Webb, of whom he says:

> He still conceives the mass of men as persons who ought
> to be decently treated, not as persons who ought freely
> to organise their own conditions of life;   in short,
> his conception of a new social order is still that of
> an order that is ordained from without, and not reali-
> sed from within (Cole, 1918).

This is not the place to go into the details of Cole's
plans for a participatory society, interesting though they
are in suggesting a blue-print for a totally participatory
society.   It is sufficient to note that Cole centres participation on the work-place, with some subsequent modifications to take in, for instance, neighbourhood-based participation.   He seems to assume that by some pluralist
balancing of the different groups the resources of society
and its social arrangements will conform to principles of
equitable distribution.   It is true that at the apex of
the complex system of regional communes and guilds there
is to be a National Commune, but as Cole conceives it this
is to be a purely co-ordinating body which will not adju-
dicate in any way between the policy decisions of other
bodies coming to it.   This is largely because he does not
envisage any conflicts between groups once a participatory

system is established.   This assumption of harmonious decision-making is, however, as several critics have pointed out (Wright, 1979, p. 66f;   Gutmann, 1980, p. 203f), quite unfounded, with the result that Cole's suggested participatory machinery is severely flawed, for any democratic society will want some means of resolving conflicts equitably when they arise.

It is interesting to note, parenthetically, that Gramsci's ideas for factory councils give rise to a similar theoretical problem to that arising within Cole's Guild Socialism.   There are important differences of course, in that Gramsci was working out his ideas within the Marxist tradition and for him the establishment of factory councils was a transitional phase on the way to the fully communist society.   It was not, so to speak, conceived as a desirable end in itself.   Gramsci, however, saw the factory councils as complemented by a political party which would provide general leadership and organizational co-ordination in the struggle against the bourgeois state.   Indeed he felt that the final failure of the councils which were established in factories in Northern Italy (they never anyway conformed exactly to Gramsci's theoretical blue-print and he always referred to them as the 'nucleus' or 'embryo' of the fully-developed council) was a result of the lack of an experienced, developed political party to co-ordinate grassroots efforts.   Clearly Gramsci was concerned with a revolutionary strategy, but his problem of the relationship between the party and the councils exemplifies the recurring difficulty for participatory theorists (whether within a democratic framework or not) of how the decisions and policies of the many grassroots decision-making bodies can be equitably incorporated into an overall policy for the whole society.   To say that Gramsci recognized this problem is not to say that he solved it, since it is not at all clear how in his system the councils and the party are to be organizationally related without the party adopting the elitist role which Gramsci explicitly rejected (see Boggs's comments, 1976, pp. 95f;   and also Kolakowski, 1978, pp. 244-52).

More recently, in the last chapter of The Life and Times of Liberal Democracy, Macpherson attempts a sketch of a participatory democracy which sets out very clearly how the different decision-making bodies are to relate to one another.   In his view such a system must take a pyramidal form, with direct democracy at the base and delegate democracy at every level above that.   Thus, he says:

one would start with direct democracy at the neighbourhood or factory level - actual face-to-face discussion
and decision by consensus or majority, and election of
delegates who would make up a council at the next more
inclusive level, say a city borough or ward or a town-
ship.   The delegates would have to be sufficiently in-
structed by and accountable to those who elected them
to make decisions at the council level reasonably democratic.   So it would go on up to the top level, which
would be a national council for matters of national
concern, and local and regional councils for matters of
less than national concern.   At whatever level beyond
the smallest primary one the final decisions on different matters were made, the issues would certainly have
to be formulated by a committee of the council.   Thus,
at whatever level the reference up stopped, it would
stop in effect with a small committee of that level's
council.   This may seem a far cry from democratic control.   But I think it is the best we can do.   What is
needed, at every stage, to make the system democratic,
is that the decision-makers and issue-formulators elected from below be held responsible to those below by
being subject to re-election or even recall (Macpherson, 1977, pp. 108-9).

Macpherson then outlines three situations in which such a
pyramidal councils system will not work, but suggests
that, if these situations can be avoided, there is no flaw
inherent in the system which should make it fail.   If the
situation is not an immediately post-revolutionary one,
not a deeply class-divided one, and not one in which the
mass of the people are apathetic, there is every reason
for the pyramidal councils system to work.   Macpherson
then discusses an approximation to this model since there
is no space in it for political parties.   It is likely
that any Western society which attempted to move towards
such a participatory structure would do so not via a one-
party system but via a multi-party system, perhaps ini-
tially via a coalition of social-democratic and socialist
parties.   Macpherson therefore considers the problem of
how far participatory structures are compatible with a
competitive party system.   His conclusion is finally that
'genuinely participatory parties ... could operate through
a parliamentary or congressional structure to provide a
substantial measure of participatory democracy' (Macpherson, 1977, p. 114).   Leaving aside the approximate model,
it seems to me that Macpherson's full-blown model exhibits
serious flaws.   At first sight it appears to overcome the
problem noted in Cole and Gramsci of how grassroots deci-

sions are to be related to a society-wide policy.   In one
sense, indeed, it does do this.   It is very clear how the
decisions on the various sub-bodies are to be passed up
through the system so that a decision necessarily emerges
from the national council, either from consensus or as a
resulted of a majority vote.   There is therefore an
implementable decision which has come from the grassroots
decision-making bodies; it is not clear, for different
reasons, that there would be one in the Cole and Gramsci
arrangements.   There is, however, a problem with Macpherson's model.

In the process of feeding decisions upwards from lower
to ever higher bodies, it could be the case that the preferences of some people are always voted out.   On almost
every issue some people may always be in the minority.
They may be easily identifiable minorities, the old in a
predominantly youthful society, or less identifiable ones,
people who are concerned about noise pollution in a
robustly boisterous society.   At this point one could
take two possible stances.   One might argue that this
state of affairs would be unfortunate but, sadly, must be
regarded as an unavoidable fact of life once all the
appropriate procedures for decision-making have been
observed.   This may, however, be to give up too soon,
especially if one accepts the arguments in Chapter one
about the majority vote as an exercise of power over the
minority.   Alternatively one may feel that the situation
described is unrealistic in a democracy because those participating at the various levels would not be voting
'selfishly' but in the public interest.   Even if, however, one accepts for the moment the distinction between
selfish voting and public interest voting, it does not
help, unless one also assumes that decisions about the
public interest will somehow be unanimous.   Without that
assumption the majority/minority problem simply arises
again.   The only answer, it seems to me, is to accept
something like the Macpherson participatory structure on a
neighbourhood basis but to build into it constitutional
constraints which secure to the individual certain rights
which are not overridable.   I am, of course, not claiming that this will totally solve the majority/minority
problem.   There will be occasions when minorities will
not get what they want.   What I am advocating is a bill
of rights to secure at least basic needs, defined in terms
of the 'primary goods' mentioned in Chapter one.   This
idea of a participatory structure with constitutional constraints securing to the individual certain rights is very
close to Amy Gutmann's 'incomplete sketch of the core

governmental framework required by any democratic and
egalitarian society' (Gutmann, 1980, p. 202).   It is not,
however, identical with her account, even in its major
points.   It will be clearest, therefore, if I present it
as an independent account, referring from time to time to
points Gutmann makes.

Let me start, first, with the basic rights which must
be secured to every citizen by the constitutional framework.   These are related, as I say, to the 'primary
goods' listed in Chapter one.

(i)   In line with the points made about wealth at the end
of Chapter one, each citizen will have a right to a basic
minimum of welfare provision.   The level will vary
between different historically situated societies but,
unless extreme circumstances dictate this, it will not be
a bare minimum sufficient only to support life at subsistence level but what is judged appropriate to a decent
human life.   This will of course involve a number of
judgments of value at various points.   However the need
to make such judgments does not in itself constitute a
reason to avoid coming to some judgment about the require-
ments for a decent human life in a given historical situation.   In addition there will be a framework for permissible income variations written into the constitutional
framework (see Chapter one, p. 31).   Within this broad
framework it will be possible to make recommendations for
appropriate incomes for different jobs if the society
wishes to do this, perhaps because, for instance, it
decides to use this method to motivate people towards certain jobs rather than others.   Written into the constitutional framework, too, will be a provision for citizens to
determine the assignment of surplus wealth to private
individuals and/or to public projects as they deem best.

(ii)   Citizens will also have certain constitutional
rights where opportunities are concerned.   They will have
a right to a basic education in a democratic setting and a
right to sample as many further perspectives, ways of life
and activities as their society is able to make available.
What is implied in more detail by this right in both
formal and informal education, as also the rationale for
it, are developed in Chapters three, four and five.

Other 'opportunity' rights guaranteed by the constitution will largely be of a negative sort, i.e. rights which
lay down that the citizen shall not be discriminated
against in respect of employment, enjoyment of leisure
facilities, etc., on grounds of race, sex or religion.

(iii)   Citizens will also be guaranteed constitutional rights with respect to freedom of thought and expression.

(iv)   Citizens will also have the right to protection by the rule of law, with an independent judiciary guaranteeing their other rights by this means.

(v)   Finally citizens will have the constitutional right to participate in the exercise and control of power whether this is in their work-place, or neighbourhood, or in some society-wide forum.

What I have termed constitutional rights constitute the very framework of the democratic society and in their most basic form can only be changed by near-unanimous consent of the citizens.   The right to minimum welfare provision, to equal opportunities, to freedom of thought and expression, the rule of law and the equal right to participate in the exercise and control of power fall into this category, although rights deriving from these and formulated with respect to the conditions prevailing within historically situated societies (e.g. the right to a particular income for a particular job within the permitted scale of incomes) may be changed with considerably less than unanimous consent.   This is not the place to specify what level of consent is appropriate to different kinds of rights: I simply want to make this crude distinction to underline the necessarily entrenched position of the constitutional rights as underpinnings of the democratic society.

The institutional complement of the basic constitutional framework set out above is a national representative forum to which members are elected on the basis of one person, one vote.   Such an institution is necessary if decisions affecting the whole society are to be made, in the light of the basic constitutional framework, for the whole society.   In this I agree with Amy Gutmann who, suggesting such a forum, says:

The choice among candidates should be considered by citizens a choice based upon the criterion of 'judicial competence':   Each citizen should ask who will most justly interpret the spirit of the constitution in particular cases ... national representatives are not to see themselves simply as mandated delegates of their constituencies.   They are to be interpreters of the constitution and representatives of the public good first and of the particular interests of their constit-

uencies second, as far as is consistent with the interests of society as an egalitarian whole (Gutmann, 1980,
p. 200).

In implementing such a structure questions arise about the
sphere of competence and responsibility of this central
body vis-à-vis those of the other participatory organizations.   The division of labour is in one sense fairly
clear.   Matters which are the exclusive concern of groups
within the society and which have negligible repercussions
on the wider society (e.g. decisions to do with some
aspects of services provided by local police forces, hospitals, civil service departments, etc.) will be decided
at local level, while matters which affect the whole
society (e.g. decisions to do with defence, with society-
wide income differentials, with aspects of policing policy
which apply to all areas) will eventually come for decision to the national forum, which will have the decisions
of the local and regional participatory organizations in
some summary form before it.

This suggested structure does not assume a consensus on
major policy decisions (as Cole seems to), nor does it
cast the national forum in an elitist role (Gramsci's
problem), nor does it simply give the ultimate body a
rubber-stamping role, always endorsing the majority decision.   This is clear if we examine two different cases
which may come to the national forum for decision.   The
first is one in which the combined decisions of various
participatory organizations in the society would, if put
into effect, involve discrimination in relation to job
opportunities.   Perhaps they are such as to exclude women
or West Indians from certain jobs.   Here, in the light of
the constitutional rights listed, the national forum will
simply veto the proposed policy.   It violates the constitutional rights under (ii) designed to secure all members
of the society certain 'primary goods'.

The second case is more interesting because less
straightforward.   The national forum has to make a decision on a matter in which preferences in the society are
divided between different policies, where none of those
policies would involve a violation of constitutional
rights.   Perhaps, for instance, a majority want income
differentials whereas a minority want flat equality with
other kinds of incentives to lure people into unattractive
jobs.   In such a case the national forum has a duty to
make sure that the implications of the two policies are
clear to citizens, but, after people fully understand the

likely effects of the two policies, in many cases it
simply has to follow the preferences of the majority.
Not always, however.   In the case of some preference
clashes it may be able to suggest some compromise policy
which attempts to cater equitably for all interests.
There may, alternatively, be some way of making special
provision for minority interests, whilst implementing the
majority decision.   The democratic society is, after all,
steadfastly opposed to endorsing one conception of the
good life over another in its policies and will want its
national decision-making body to use whatever judgment and
ingenuity it possesses so to arrange matters as to allow
individuals to realize their own conceptions of the good
life.   It is, as well, an elected body and if its compromise decisions or special arrangements are not acceptable
to the electorate, its members will not be re-elected.
If, however, it is successful in upholding constitutional
rights and arriving at acceptable solutions where permissible preferences clash, it will be acting in the spirit
of the constitution and for the public good, because the
public good in such a society involves, _inter alia_, promoting the basic principles of democracy to ensure as far
as possible that individuals' conceptions of the good life
can be realized.

There is a problem, however, as Amy Gutmann recognizes,
in choosing individuals who display 'judicial competence'
and who can be relied upon to interpret the spirit of the
constitution and represent the public good.   She thinks
we must presume the 'potential judicial attributes of all
citizens' (Gutmann, 1980, p. 200).   We must not forget,
however, the role of education in such a society.   Liberals are sometimes accused of using education like glue to
make stick political proposals which rest on an optimistic
view of human beings.   Perhaps, however, in a case like
this that is the role for education.   The important question is only whether education can perform it.   In Chapter three I give some reasons for thinking it can.

PARTICIPATION IN THE WORK-PLACE

It was suggested in Chapter one that in a society aspiring
to be a full democracy appropriate democratic arrangements
would have to be extended beyond what is conventionally
regarded as the political sphere to the work-place.   This
has been assumed, too, in the immediately preceding section.   What would constitute 'appropriate democratic
arrangements'?

My initial concern is with the internal democratic
structure of work-places and not with their accountability
to the wider society.   We touched on issues of accountability in an earlier point about local and national monitoring of, for instance, policing policies and towards the
end of this section we shall be considering them again,
because issues of internal democracy are inextricably
linked with the democratic relationship of work-places to
the wider community.   Let us, however, focus first on a
number of suggestions which have been made for rendering
the internal structure of work-places democratic.

Work-place democracy equals the existence of strong trade
unions

There is a persistent view that all the fuss about extending democracy to the work-place, attempting to devise
schemes of greater worker-participation, investigating the
desirability and feasibility of worker-co-operatives is
really rather beside the point: if we take the trouble to
look around our actual empirical democracy, we shall find
that we have adequate work-place democracy now.   A
notable exponent of this view is Professor H. Clegg (1951,
1960).   For Clegg what is crucial to the notion of political democracy is the existence of an official opposition
so that the electorate may choose between men and parties.
The mirror-image of the official opposition party (parties) in the political sphere is the strong trade union in
the industrial sphere.   If we have strong trade unions
opposing management we have industrial democracy.

This account of work-place democracy can, it seems to
me, be dismissed fairly briskly.   First, as the sole criterion for the existence of democracy an official opposition is certainly not sufficient and may not be necessary.
It is not sufficient, for one can point to historical
examples where an official opposition has existed but the
political system has not been a democratic one.   One
example would be the UK before the series of reform acts
which extended the suffrage in the nineteenth century.
Further, an official opposition party (parties) may not
even be necessary to democracy as long as policies can be
opposed by dissenting groups or individuals.   This would
allow small-scale groups, e.g. consumers' co-operatives,
to be democratic even if they do not, as they almost certainly will not, contain organized opposition parties.
But even if one granted Clegg's point that to have an
organized opposition is to have democracy, his position is

an untenable one because the crucial point about organized
opposition parties is that they can replace the government, if the electorate so chooses.   This a trade union
cannot do.   Clegg even recognizes this, he says: 'The
trade union is thus industry's opposition - an opposition
which can never become a government' (Clegg, 1951, p. 22).
He does not seem to realize that with this admission his
whole argument collapses.

I shall not spend any longer considering the view -
surely a non-starter - that strong trade unions constitute
fully-fledged industrial democracy.   Anyone still finding
that view plausible I would refer to Paul Blumberg's
witheringly thorough demolition of Clegg's position in
Industrial Democracy: The Sociology of Participation
(Blumberg, 1968, Chapter 7).

Work-place democracy equals worker-directors

Another version of work-place democracy which I shall not
linger over is that found in the British Bullock report,
which I take as an example of a worker-directors' scheme.
The Bullock committee, constrained by its terms of reference only to consider 'the need for a radical extension of
industrial democracy in the control of companies by means
of representation on boards of directors, and accepting
the essential role of trade union organisations in this
process' (my emphasis) (Bullock, 1977, p. v) came out, in
these circumstances, with predictable recommendations.
The main suggestion which concerns us was that in enterprises with more than 2,000 employees new joint boards
should be established which would reduce the existing sole
power of shareholders over a company's affairs, although
the shareholders would retain the right to veto certain
matters such as acquisition and sales of company assets.
The new boards would be constituted according to a 2 x + y
formula.   This would mean that the 2 'x' groups, shareholders and employee representatives (chosen through trade
union machinery) would each have an equal number of representatives and they would jointly choose a third 'y' group
which would be an odd number greater than one, but smaller
than x.   (The Report suggests that the 'y' group could be
representatives of senior management or experts like
solicitors, bankers or full-time trade union officials.)

How far can these proposals be seen as an extension of
democracy to the industrial sphere?   Despite the fierce
opposition they provoked from employers' federations,

banks and other City interests, they must be judged, I
think, as a very minimal extension of democratic forms
into industrial life.

Although superficially such a scheme of union-based
worker-directors looks somewhat like an extension of representative democracy into the industrial sphere, it is
clearly more unlike than like.   Elected representatives
in the political sphere, although remote from those who
elected them as the worker-directors are not, do at least
exercise sovereign political power on behalf of the electorate.   The worker-directors have no comparable power.
Considerable power, amounting to the power of veto in some
cases, is still held by the shareholders.   Worker-directors are merely one voice on the board, one influence on
any policy.   In response it might be argued that this is
wholly democratic as the shareholders have an interest too
since they are putting up the capital.   But why should
the contribution of capital rather than labour give one
ultimate power over an enterprise?   What makes the contribution of money to an enterprise more significant than
time, energy, ingenuity, perhaps, in some cases, even
health?   (These questions raise in turn another question
to which we shall have to return.   This is the question
of the type of ownership appropriate to a fully-fledged
system of work-place democracy.)

Even if the worker-directors system could escape the
above objection, it still would not necessarily represent
a thorough-going example of work-place democracy.   For
such a system of worker-directors could be compatible with
a rigid determination of the day-to-day running of the
enterprise in every minute particular from the top.   It
could be consistent with a policy which treated individual
employees as so many more or less reluctant bodies to be
shunted around or manipulated as seemed to be most efficient.   Such a system of worker-directors, in other
words, need be no particular respecter of the autonomy of
the mass of the individual workers as moral agents.

The Bullock report recommendations, then - taken as one
example of a worker-directors' scheme - fall short as
institutional embodiments of democratic values.

Work-place democracy equals workers' co-operatives

Perhaps a more promising organization, democratically
speaking, is the workers' co-operative, for an enterprise

run by its work-force would seem to represent the ultimate
in the institutionalization of moral autonomy, in that the
work-force determines the organization and policies of the
enterprise.   Certainly there were many who thought so in
the period 1910-22, in the heyday of syndicalism and Guild
Socialism.   In the 1970s a number of worker-co-operatives
were established in the UK, though often in slightly
dismal circumstances as a last-ditch stand against redun-
dancy.   There are also more longstanding examples in the
UK and elsewhere, probably the most well known being the
Mondragon co-operatives in Spain (see, e.g., Oakeshott,
1978, Chapter 10).

   Doubts about the desirability of worker-co-operatives
have, however, been raised by Robert Nozick (1974, Chapter
8).   Nozick first questions the likelihood of long-term
investment in a workers' co-operative since workers will
have little incentive to invest in long-term projects on
which they will see no return.   Secondly, he suggests
that if profits are to be shared amongst workers, it may
be in their interests to prevent the growth of the work-
force so as to maximize average profits per worker rather
than total profits.   Finally, he points out that there
may be great discrepancies in pay between workers doing
basically the same jobs in different co-operatives.   The
first two points rest, it is true, on a rather pessimistic
view of human nature and the possibilities of political
education, but let us for the moment take them at face
value.   Certainly the force of Nozick's three points is
to suggest that a system of worker-co-operatives would fit
uneasily into a democratic society.   It could in fact
become a society composed of numerous producer groups,
each characterized by a spirit of corporate selfishness.
The problem is that the very structure institutionalizes
group selfishness.   Why should the workers making a particular product have total control over what they make and
how they invest?   What about the consumer's voice and the
voices of all members of the community in what they want
produced and how they want communal resources used?
Independent worker-co-operatives may guarantee the autonomy of their work-force but at the expense of the autonomy
of the rest of the community.

Work-place democracy equals state control of the economy

Is the next logical move state control of the economy with
planning from the centre by democratically elected representatives?   Here the problem for democracy - there may

of course be other problems too! - is that when authority
is exercised from outside the work-place in the interests
of the whole community the position of the individual
worker can be as morally depressed as under the most rigid
system of individual control and ownership.   She may have
no say in the organization of her work-place and no recog-
nition of her autonomy as a moral agent.

Work-place democracy equals worker-co-operatives plus
community policy co-ordination

If we put together the last two possibilities, we arrive
at a demand for machinery reminiscent of that described in
the preceding section for the society as a whole.
Workers of all kinds, in industry and in other organizations, hospitals, libraries, shops and so on have primary
responsibility for the internal running of their own concerns.   They must determine a form of democratic machinery for the management of the enterprise which enshrines
the values of autonomy and justice and allows for equal
access to the exercise, or control, of power.   This will
undoubtedly be different in different contexts, though enshrining the same values.   For this reason it is impossible to say anything in general about the kind of machinery that might evolve, except of course that it will
always involve processes of consultation and accountability.   At the same time the community oversees the general
development of such institutions to guarantee that the
public interest is not overlooked.   Two kinds of policies
contrary to the public interest might otherwise occur.

First, policies in the broadly economic area which
might infringe constitutional rights.   The need to protect these rights is the reason, as we saw in the last
section, for establishing the national forum.   That forum
would be as concerned with the infringement of rights in
the economic sphere as in any other, as indeed the previous examples about income differentials and employment
policies indicated.

The second sort of policy, whilst not infringing constitutional rights, might well be contrary to the public
interest when considered, not in isolation, but in the
light of other policies.   The need for a body (or bodies)
to oversee community development for this reason has been
underlined by the work of a number of people, including
Barry and Hirsch (Barry, 1965;   Hirsch, 1977).   It is
easy to demonstrate, for instance, that for some particular

individual in the UK rationally considering her situation,
the decision to buy a motor car seems a sensible one which
will make life more pleasurable, comfortable and convenient.   If enough people make that decision, though, as we
know, roads are choked, journeys take longer than envisaged, there is air pollution, medical services need to be
expanded to cope with road accident victims, and so on.
This is one of the many examples that could be adduced
where millions of 'sensible' decisions, discretely made,
do not necessarily produce a desirable situation from the
point of view of the whole community, including the original 'sensible' chooser.   Consideration of this case suggests that a community transport policy would be prefer-
able to a situation where any workers' co-operative can
simply set up in business to make motor cars, motor
scooters, helicopters or what you will to try and attract
individual consumers.

The proposal is, then, for the extension of democracy
into the work-place by means of self-governing workers'
co-operatives with some machinery for community policy
oversight and co-ordination (the national forum or some
sub-committee of it) to protect constitutional rights and
the public interest.

Participation in the work-place: two problems

Such is the general framework of machinery for the extension of democracy into the work-place.   It may be thought,
however, to raise more intractable problems than participatory democracy in what is traditionally regarded as the
political sphere proper.

First, the problem of ownership.   What form of ownership is compatible with participatory democracy in the
economic sphere?   More concretely, who owns the worker-
co-operatives?   Can the workers composing them own them
or must the community own them?   This raises questions
about the justification for individual groups of workers
owning such social goods as the resources and means of
production of the enterprise in which they work.   There
is no need to go over again the problems of determining
exactly what kinds of goods may, or may not, be owned by
individuals in a participatory democracy (see Chapter one,
p. 31f).   But aside from the general moral issues raised
by the question of ownership, a particular problem emerges
in a system in which individual workers own the co-operative.   This is because part of the understanding of what

it is to own something is that the owner has ultimate control over the thing owned.   She can, after all, refuse to
allow others to use it or continue using it.   This being
so, an individual in a co-operative who wanted to leave it
would have the right to take her share, even if this seriously damaged the enterprise.   Such problems can be avoided if the community owns the resources and means of production and leases them to the workers.   So, for this
practical reason alone, community ownership with the co-
operatives leasing resources would probably be the preferred mode of ownership.   In a situation, however, when
talk of ownership in the conventional sense, as we saw in
Chapter one, may not be appropriate at all, it would be
foolish to claim that only one form of ownership is possible in a participatory democracy.   As Dahl says of the
Yugoslav situation:

> no one owns the enterprise.   It is not, certainly,
> owned by the state or by shareholders.   It is not
> owned by the workers in the enterprise.   The point is
> that 'property' is a bundle of rights.   Once the
> pieces in this bundle have been parcelled out, nothing
> exactly corresponding to the conventional meaning of
> ownership or property remains (Dahl's emphasis) (Dahl,
> 1970, p. 132).

In the light of Dahl's caution about too readily attempting to apply conventional notions of ownership to the participatory situation, it seems to me that leasing of resources from the community is permissible but other forms
of ownership may be too.   The acid test must be whether
any given form is compatible with the kind of self-management and community policy co-ordination argued for earlier.

A related problem arises from the market economy.   Is
the latter compatible with the kind of participatory democracy described?   Influenced by David Miller (1977), I am
persuaded that at least a modified form of it may be;
indeed that it may be essential for the realization of
some democratic values.   Let me explain.   I take it to
be basic to the idea of the market that decisions to produce goods or services are made not by some authority but
by the producers themselves with a view to selling to cus-
tomers who have no obligation to buy from them.   In the
kind of democracy I have described the initiative for the
setting up of a co-operative would come in the main from
individuals who would probably be leased the means of production from the state and set up in business, attempting
to make a profit from selling in the open market.   I say

'in the main', because as I have indicated there would
have to be the possibility of community control over the
provision of goods and services.   Profits would be taxed
to build up resources for the community and to finance a
welfare state.   Co-operatives unable to make a profit,
and which there were no public interest reasons for supporting either in the short or longer term, would clearly
fold up.   Their members would receive some kind of unem-
ployment benefit until they were either able to find a
more profitable line of production or move into other co-
operatives.   Such a market system allows for individual
initiative, flair and ingenuity in producing goods in a
way in which non-market public ownership systems do not.
Those, in practice, often over-produce unwanted goods and
foster black market systems.   The market system in the
participatory democracy allows for the exercise of imagi-
native business flair extolled by businessmen in our ·
present society but without the morally obnoxious motivations often associated with that in practice - the desire
for individual aggrandizement, for instance, or the desire
to exercise power over others ('I run 26 women and girls
now,' as a production manager in a small firm proudly said
to me).   Here the motivations are rather different, the
desire to make a profit for the community generally, to
enhance the quality of life in it and the satisfaction of
working with others on a project which has been jointly
planned, developed and organized.

Participation in the work-place: three objections

There are a number of possible objections to the exten-
sions of participatory democracy to the work-place.   Let
me consider three.

(i)   The first springs from what is taken to be a crip-
pling paradox in this position.   The argument for work-
place democracy is based on the assumption that moral
autonomy is a value fundamental to democracy which must be
enshrined in relations in the work-place as it is in democratic government.   So far so good, a critic might argue,
but the proposals advanced here, far from enshrining autonomy, are more likely to destroy it.

   If everyone is to be herded into co-operatives what
about the autonomy of the person who enjoys working alone,
running a business, say, single-handedly?   I am thinking
of the taxi driver, peanut seller, flute teacher or what
you will who finds a certain satisfaction in her indepen-

dent mode of life precisely because she values the autonomy it gives her.   Here, however, I see no problem and no
paradox.

Individuals who want to freelance in whatever way they
choose, can, like co-operatives, offer their wares on the
open market.   No authority relations are involved here
and my only concern is to arrive at a democratic form of
authority relations where they exist.   Here they do not.

Potentially more serious is the same objection directed
at work-place democracy where it does exist.   Here, it
might be argued, the aim is autonomy but in fact the participatory democracy would be tediously bureaucratic.
Endless consultations and meetings would sap individual
initiative and fetter autonomy.   But this need not follow
at all.   There is no question, for instance, of a central
government imposing some preconceived 'rational' framework
of committees and so on on all institutions.   Quite the
contrary.   The idea is self-management: that individual
institutions - industrial enterprises and other organizations - work out their form of management.   Within broad
guidelines from the community, an individual enterprise
determines its own organization, from the way it organizes
accountability internally to the frequency of its various
meetings.   There is nothing to suggest that this system
would be bureaucratic.   One suspects in fact that a
number of pressures would operate to keep the administration as functional as possible.   It would obviously be in
the interest of the whole work-force to have the enterprise run economically and efficiently.

(ii)   There might be an objection (noted already in Chapter one) to what might be called the 'politicizing' of
working life.   Some people, it might be argued, are not
interested in politics, they simply want to do an honest
day's work.   If, however, work-place democracy as an extension of political democracy is a moral matter, then I
have suggested the alleged fact of apathy towards politics
cannot count as an argument against introducing it.   It
will rather be a matter of getting people to realize that
they have moral duties in an area where perhaps it had not
occurred to them that they did (see Chapter one, p. 17f).

In any case I am not sure of the truth of the allega-
tion.   There seems to be considerable evidence to suggest
that whatever may be the case about national politics, as
far as having a say over working conditions·is concerned,
there is no lack of interest (Blumberg, 1968, p. 133 and
research reviewed in Chapter 5).

This leads me to draw attention to two advantages of work-place democracy.

For many people it may be a way in to a more general understanding of political matters.   As Blumberg puts it at the end of his book:

> To the extent that workers' management is successful, it enables - or rather, compels - the worker to see the narrow horizons of his minute task and to take on a greater perspective which encompasses his economic unit, his department, his factory, his industry, and, in fact the entire economy (Blumberg, 1968, p. 233).

And, he might have added, his community and its relations to other states.

Further, for some people it may even be a second chance for education more generally.   It is now a cliché to say that education is a chancy business, but given our inadequate understanding of motivation we cannot afford to ignore the possibility that involvement in work-place democracy may awaken in some people an interest in economics, history or perhaps sociology or philosophy which they would never have dreamed could have had any interest for them.

(iii) Finally, there is the question of whether the 'average working person' will be able to cope with work-place democracy.   As a recent pamphlet has it, 'Can Workers Manage?'   There is much that one could say here, but I will make just three quick points.

When this question is raised, it is often forgotten that we do actually have many examples of workers managing, in this country, in the Mondragon co-operatives and in Yugoslavia.   Unless therefore one is to argue that all these count as 'special cases', there seems to be no doubt that workers can manage.

One form of opposition to the kind of work-place democracy I have been arguing for may stem from a misunderstanding.   Some critics are opposed to any such arrangements because they see them as an irrational absurdity. How is it possible for a firm's workers to assemble round a table and, e.g., correct a design fault in Concorde, work out a new computer programme or decide on the most appropriate overseas markets for its products?   This is to assume, though, that work-place democracy implies that

there must be no experts and that each member of the work-
force must contribute to all decision-making at every
stage.   I cannot see that this is implied.   What is
implied if one is concerned to institutionalize democratic
values is something rather different: a freely working,
well-developed process of consultation and accountability.
This may take various forms, depending on the context, but
whatever precise concrete form it takes it must meet two
conditions.   First, no one, whatever her particular job
in the firm, must be debarred from making a contribution
to decision-making and indeed an ethos must prevail such
that people feel free to offer suggestions and criticisms.
Second, those involved in specialized decision-making must
be accountable to fellow members of the work-force.   I do
not pretend that it will be easy to devise machinery,
appropriate to a given context, to institutionalize such a
process of consultation and accountability and equally
difficult will be the development of attitudes of concern
for others, willingness to have one's errors pointed out
and so on which alone could allow such machinery to work.
When we can devise such machinery and encourage such
attitudes, however, Blumberg, Braverman and Edgley all
cite material to suggest that there is a vast amount of
knowledge and expertise highly relevant to grassroots
work-place democracy to be tapped.   If our present organization of work assigns people jobs which require hardly
any skill or training, it does not follow that those
people could not exercise skill or judgment.   We must not
fall into the trap of thinking that a woman spraying a toy
or filling a pickle jar can do only that (Blumberg, 1968,
Chapters 5 and 6;   Braverman, 1974;   Edgley, 1978).

Finally, the dynamic role of political education is
forgotten when people raise this question.   We have
hardly tried formal political education and even less have
we tried education for work-place democracy, so whether or
not workers can manage must, at least for the moment,
remain an open question.

DECISION-MAKING

The question of how different groups in the participatory
democracy come to decisions has been mentioned more than
once.   It is tempting to imagine that, in conditions of
equal access to power, their members will, through reasoned discussion, come to an agreed view.   But although
this may sometimes be the case, there is no guarantee of
unanimity.   Citizens can be expected to hold different

views on the priority to be given to different policies,
for instance, and although some may modify their views on
hearing the arguments for other policies, others may well
find themselves confirmed in theirs.   In the face of conflicting, considered and sincerely held views on a given
set of policy options what can be done?   In most cases
citizens cannot simply agree to differ and shelve the
decision: some policy has to be adopted and implemented.
A quick review of the possibilities suggests that where
there is conflict the most sensible course is to follow
the wishes of the majority.   What, after all, are the
alternatives?   One might insist on unanimity: but this
allows one member of the group to veto a policy desired by
all the rest.   This hardly seems defensible, since why
should one person have this power to determine affairs?
Also constant striving for unanimity on all issues would
effectively rule out any policies designed to change the
status quo, since there is a strong likelihood that there
would always be at least one person against any change.
Going by the wishes of the minority seems equally to be a
non-starter, for what grounds could be found for giving a
small group of people the power to determine the policy
for all?   This appears to leave majority preference as
the only reasonable solution.   But, as we saw in Chapter
one reasonable though majority voting may appear, grave
and worrying problems face any democrat who attempts to
justify it.   The temptation is to go for a crude justification along the lines that majority voting is the best of
a rather poor set of options because it at least satisfies
more people than it disappoints on any given policy decision.   Even leaving aside the familiar problems (some of
which are discussed below) involved in the summing up of
wants in this way, such a justification must make a democrat very uneasy.   She is, after all, committed to democracy as that form of government which can best take
account of the autonomy of the individual citizen, yet
here she has to countenance a form of machinery for decision-making which overrides the autonomous choices of the
minority.   Why are some people's autonomous choices to be
preferred to others?'   Can this be simply because more
people happen to share them?

I wish now to discuss six specific problems raised by
the majority principle.   This will lead me to qualify the
principle in various ways so that when we return to the
problem of justification, we will be dealing with a different, modified majority principle.   It will be a majority principle with some of its sharper corners knocked
off: for that reason its justification may present less
of a problem.

(i) To adopt the majority principle neat permits the possibility of majority decisions which repeal basic democratic rights.   If enough people agree, the franchise could
be limited, habeas corpus repealed, free speech outlawed,
etc. etc.   It seems clear that rights which guarantee the
democratic framework of government must be safeguarded.
The exact means of doing so need not detain us here (this
may be an appropriate place at which to demand unanimity,
or near unanimity), but it is clear that the wishes of the
majority cannot be overriding, as these could be inconsistent with the values to which democrats are committed.   A
piece of machinery like majority voting cannot be allowed
to destroy the democratic framework of society.   That
would be absurd.

Someone may raise the reasonable objection that democrats would not want to destroy the democratic framework.
That is surely true in the abstract, but when people feel
strongly about _particular_ issues they may sometimes be
prepared to vote for partial infringements of fundamental
rights and in some circumstances contribute unintentionally
to the piecemeal dismantling of the democratic framework.
The best way for democrats to protect themselves against
witting, or unwitting, attacks on the framework is to make
the basic democratic rights (i.e., the rights securing
access to the primary goods), constitutional rights and as
such immune from majority voting procedures.   Making constitutional rights immune in this way deals with the familiar problem, raised, for instance, by Bernard Williams
(1973, p. 105), of the possibility of a majority depriving
a racial minority of their rights.   First and foremost,
then, the across-the-board application of the majority
principle must be restricted in the interests of safe-
guarding democratic values (Pennock, 1979, p. 378 makes a
similar point).

(ii) We have already touched on the use of majority
voting procedures for decisions between preferences.   In
Chapter one we imagined a community with resources for one
type of leisure facility only choosing between a swimming
pool and a theatre.   We raised the question, why, given a
view of democracy which lays stress on the moral autonomy
of individual citizens, one should give more weight to
that view which simply happens to be shared by more citizens.

It might be argued that even those whose policy choice
was not implemented still had their choices _considered_ and
that majority voting is consistent with democratic values,

particularly egalitarian values, in taking the considered
preferences of each person each to count for one.   As I
pointed out in Chapter one, however, a problem of injustice still remains (there I talked about it in terms of an
exercise of power, p. 28f),in that the majority has its
preferences considered and implemented and the minority
only has its preferences considered (and not implemented).
This is problem enough.   But the injustice can be further
compounded.   It may well be the case that even the egalitarian consideration of all preferences is corrupted by
the presence of 'external' preferences, as Dworkin has
called them.   Dworkin, in the paper 'Reverse Discrimination' (Dworkin, 1977), distinguishes between 'personal'
preferences - preferences a person may have for his own
enjoyment of goods or opportunities - and 'external' preferences - preferences a person may have for the assignment
of goods or opportunities to others.   In considering the
community's choice between the swimming pool and theatre,
up to this point I have presented the case as if each
member were voting according to his or her personal preference ('I can see plenty of drama on television, I will
vote for the swimming pool! etc. etc.).   But it may not
be like this, I may not have any personal preference for
either the swimming pool or the theatre: for whatever
reasons I may not envisage myself ever using either facility.   But I may well cast my vote in favour of the swimming pool because I would enjoy seeing firm-bodied
athletic people strolling around the town, their graceful
postures the result of much use of the swimming pool.
Here, because of my liking for athletic-looking people,
the swimmers are getting an extra vote.   The contest is
not, therefore, a straightforward one between personal
preferences: external preferences are entering in too.
The chance of anyone getting his or her personal preference is going to depend in part on how many people esteem
or like him or her, or his or her way of life.   This is a
corruption of the original rationale for majority voting
where each vote supposedly counts for one.

I must admit that I am at a loss to know how to tackle
the problem of external preferences.   There seems to be
no foolproof way of detecting external preferences and
discounting them. (2)   Is the only safeguard political
education?   Clearly it can be a task within political
education to point out the problem posed by external preferences in a democratic community, where the extent to
which others esteem one's choices should not have the
power to determine whether or not those choices are implemented.   Within such an education people can be invited

to reflect on the problem of external preferences and, when they have no personal preference on an issue, to consider abstaining from the vote.   If people still wish to exercise external preferences, however, there seems to be no machinery which can be brought into play to weed out such preferences.   Not unless, that is, one can use a piece of machinery which has been suggested to deal with the connected problem of intensity of preference.

The person who, as far as personal preference is concerned, is indifferent on an issue is obviously in the exactly opposite situation from the person who feels intensely on some issue.   They are at opposite ends of a continuum of feeling.   The problem of devising democratic decision-making machinery to take account of intensity of preference has exercised political theorists for some time.   Various suggestions have been made for machinery which might be sensitive to different intensities of feeling amongst different voters.   Pennock mentions an ingenious device by which individuals might register the strength of their feelings on a given issue.   He suggests that individuals might be given a 'quantum of votes' which they could then distribute as they preferred, perhaps at the extreme using them all on one issue (Pennock, 1979, p. 416, note 3).   Pennock does not go into details, about for instance the number of votes that individuals might be given in relation to the number of issues to be decided, and there is certainly no need for us to do so.   Use of this device, it seems to me, might go some way to coping with the problem of external preferences.   One might hypothesize (and what follows can be no more than a hypothesis) that if individuals had such a quiver of votes they might tend to husband them for use on issues in which they had a personal interest rather than let them loose on issues where the outcome was a matter of personal indifference to them.   Although, therefore, the intrusion of external preferences would always be a possibility, in practice this might reduce their incidence.   Even if, however, the quantum of votes suggestion proves to be unworkable, we should try, by whatever means we can devise, to modify the majority principle to take account of the linked problems of external preferences and intensity of feeling.

(iii)   A phenomenon associated with majority voting is the 'pork-barrel'.   This term labels the well-documented tendency of elected bodies (e.g. the US Congress) to vote for benefits for particular groups in excess of what is justifiable.   This occurs when two conditions obtain.   First

when representatives, to achieve a majority and secure a
benefit, must have the co-operation of others with no
interest in the benefit.   Perhaps, for instance, the representatives of some locality are anxious to ensure that
there is a decision to vote resources to enlarge its har-
bour because this will bring employment to the area.
Representatives of other localities may be persuaded to
vote for this project on the understanding that they will
be supported in some future vote to secure some benefit
for their constituents.   This is the practice of log-
rolling.   The second condition necessary for the pork-
barrel obtains when the benefits go to determinate groups
and the costs are borne by the general taxpayer.   When
this is the case support for particular projects is easy
to come by because the benefits are highly visible to the
beneficiaries and the costs not so visible to the general
taxpayer.

No democrat wants this kind of waste of resources and
whilst keeping the practice of majority voting there are
at least two ways of combating it.   The first, as with
(ii), is political education.   Log-rolling is accepted in
large part because people are unaware of its tendency to
overprovide goods at the expense of increased costs to
citizens as taxpayers.   Increased awareness of the hidden
costs of 'I'll scratch your back, if you scratch mine'
would probably go a long way towards eradicating it.
Secondly, the national forum argued for earlier (see Chapter one), with representatives acting as protectors of the
constitution and concerned for the public interest, would
also serve as a check on the policies coming from the representatives of the particular constituencies.   It would
be the specific responsibility of the national forum, as a
kind of second chamber, to judge the policies arrived at
by those interested parties from the point of view of the
public interest.

It is possible in principle, then, to check the problems of overprovision and waste sometimes caused by majority voting by both educational and constitutional means.

(iv)   It might be thought that if instead of voting indi-
vidualistically or with sectional interests in mind people
cast their votes according to what policy they thought was
in the public interest, there would be no question of
minorities having their preferences overruled.   This
would only be so, however, if people could agree unani-
mously on what policy was in the public interest.   People
do not agree on this.   One is left with majority and

minority opinions on what is in the public interest, so
the problem does not go away but just reappears in another
place.

(v) We have assumed so far that whatever difficulties
there may be with majority voting, at least after a vote
on any given issue we shall know clearly and unequivocally
what the majority wants.   This, however, may not be so.
We may be confronted by Condorcet's paradox, which gets
application when no policy is the clear favourite of 51
per cent of the voters and minority factions so disagree
as to the relative merits of policies A, B and C that each
gets one first-place vote, one second-place vote and one
third-place vote, as indicated in Table 1.

Table 1

		Voting factions		
		1	2	3
Order	First choice	A	B	C
of	Second choice	B	C	A
preference	Third choice	C	A	B

Ackerman explains clearly how it is possible in this situation to get three different answers to the question 'What
does the majority want?'

> An inspection of the matrix indicates that two groups
> of statesmen [voters] (1 and 3) will vote for A in
> preference to B; that two (1 and 2) will prefer B to
> C; and that two (2 and 3) prefer C to A.   In this
> situation, the winning program [policy] will be deter-
> mined by the group in charge of parliamentary proce-
> dure.   If the citizenry is first required to choose
> between B and C, B will emerge victorious, with groups
> 1 and 2 voting against 3.   If B is then paired against
> A, A will be victorious, with groups 1 and 3 voting
> against 2.   In contrast, if A and C are first put up
> to the voters, A will be defeated on the initial vote;
> C emerges victorious from the first round of balloting
> only to be defeated by B on the second round, with 1
> and 2 voting against 3!   And it is easy to specify yet
> another order of balloting where C emerges as 'the'
> majority winner' (Ackerman's emphasis) (Ackerman, 1980,
> p. 290).

The Condorcet paradox situation does not yield a clear-cut
answer to the question of what the majority wants.
Furthermore it provides an opportunity for an individual
or a group to exert unjustified power over others by man-
ipulating the agenda so that her or their preferred policy
achieves a majority of votes.   Ackerman's proposal for a
random-number machine to arrange the order in which A, B
and C will be paired against each other deals with the
problem of agenda manipulation at the expense of making
what emerges as 'the' majority decision on policy a matter
of chance.

(vi) So far we have been looking at the problems and difficulties which arise if we conceive of people voting
according to their preferences, leaving out of account any
question of what is morally right.   A new and different
order of problem arises if we conceive of people voting,
as Wollheim puts it (Wollheim, 1962), according to their
evaluations, that is for that policy which they think is
the best one or the one which morally ought to be pursued.
As Wollheim admits, this is a 'somewhat harsh' distinction,
since of course there are connections between wants and
evaluations, but these need not detain us now.

The problem, simply stated, is this.   I may reflect
earnestly on the many relevant considerations and sincerely come to the view that some particular policy, say a
policy of positive discrimination for women and blacks in
educational and job opportunities, is the morally right
one.   I am also, however, a democrat, committed to the
principle that where opinion on policy is divided one
should follow the decision of the majority.   In this case
let us suppose that the majority are resolutely opposed to
positive discrimination.   Given my two beliefs, about the
desirability of positive discrimination and the desirability of following the majority decision, I find myself
forced to be a highly inconsistent person.   At 11.10 am,
say, I am committed to positive discrimination, yet at
11.20 am, following the majority decision, I am committed
to a policy which roundly rejects it.   Can democrats
afford to adopt the majority principle if it involves them
in this kind of extreme inconsistency?   The argument
throughout has been for democracy as the appropriate
social arrangement for morally autonomous human agents.
But how can this be if one of its prominent decision-
making procedures will often involve individuals in a
morally unacceptable inconsistency of view?

Wollheim attempts three resolutions of what he regards

as the democrat's paradox.   He suggests (a) that we might
see an individual's policy choice as an _interim_ evaluation.   Interpreted in this way an individual's view is
that policy A ought to be enacted if enough others think
so too.   But this is a very odd conception of political
choice.   Often, after all, an individual will vote in a
certain way, knowing that few others will vote similarly,
but thinking that she must do so as a matter of principle.
Consider, too, that if the majority vote for policy B, on
this interpretation, the individual revises her interim
evaluation and supports policy B as that policy which
most people think is right.   The most damaging implication of this interpretation is, therefore, that it does
not really matter what view the individual takes, A or B,
since _any_ policy could get her approval - if enough other
citizens vote for it.   This clearly makes a complete non-
sense of political choice.

Alternatively, says Wollheim, one might take the view
(b) that the result of the majority vote is not a policy
which the individual morally _ought_ now to follow but one
which it would be wise or _prudent_ for her to follow.
Here there is no paradox.   The individual thinks that
policy A morally ought to be enacted but, at the same
time, believes it would be prudent to enact policy B.
The trouble with this way of resolving the paradox is that
one cannot distinguish the person prepared to go along
with democracy, perhaps to achieve power, from the genuine
democrat who believes that the policy chosen by the majority _ought_ to be enacted.

Having failed to resolve the paradox in the ways described, Wollheim attempts a quite different resolution (c)
which consists in his attempting to show that an individual's belief that policy A ought to be enacted and her
belief that policy B, the policy chosen by the majority,
ought to be enacted (where A and B are not identical) can
be quite compatible and do not lead her into a radically
inconsistent position.   He does this by positing the
existence of direct and oblique principles.   Direct principles refer to the morality of actions, policies, etc.
where these are picked out by some general descriptive ex-
pressions, e.g. positive discrimination, justice, telling
lies, etc.   Oblique principles refer to the morality of
actions picked out by some artificial property bestowed
upon them either as the result of an act of will of some
individual or in consequence of the corporate action of
some institution.   An example of a direct principle would
be 'Positive discrimination is the fairest policy'.   An

example of an oblique principle would be 'What the majority wills ought to be done'.   It is clear now that an
individual can assert that 'Policy A ought to be enacted'
as a direct principle and without inconsistency that
'Policy B ought to be enacted' as a derivation from an
oblique principle, i.e. the principle that one should
pursue the policy voted for by the majority.   Wollheim's
argument shows, if it works, that it is possible to be a
democrat committed to following the decision of the majority without being inconsistent.   I do not now want to
pursue the debate in the considerable literature on Wollheim's paper (3) because even if Wollheim's arguments
hold, they still leave the substantive moral dilemma for
the democrat who is faced with following a policy the majority thinks is right but with which she does not agree.
She may not be inconsistent, but she may be involved in a
clash of principles between a direct principle and an
oblique one.   In other words there may well be times when
the democrat, seeing to what the oblique principle of following the majority decision commits her, will judge that
another principle must, on this occasion, take precedence
over this one.   There is no reason, after all, why what
is commanded by the oblique principle of the majority
decision should take precedence over other moral duties.
It is no more than a prima facie principle.   The democrat
may therefore be involved in a clash of principles, about
whose status, thanks to Wollheim, we are now clearer.
She may have to contemplate resisting the majority decision, perhaps in the extreme case by some form of civil
disobedience.   This substantive moral dilemma I discuss
below (see p. 75f).

It is worth noting at this point that with Wollheim's
arguments we have in a sense come full circle because
although Wollheim may have shown that the democrat committed to the majority principle need not be inconsistent, we
have been given no reason why she should adopt the oblique
principle of majority decision, even as a prima facie
principle.   This is a fitting point at which to conclude
this section with the problem with which it began.

We have found no arguments wholeheartedly in favour of
majority decision-making, but neither have we found any
viable substitute for determining policy in the absence of
unanimous agreement.   The consideration of the problems
raised by majority voting - the possibility that minorities might be deprived of basic rights, the possible overprovision of goods, the inability to discriminate between
personal and external preferences and so on - suggests,

however, that its use must be qualified.   This is not
the appropriate place to go into detail on the kind of
machinery which might be used.   We have, however, considered in passing some of the kinds of devices which democrats might want to use - devices like constitutional constraints to protect civil rights, the provision of a quantum of votes for voters to distribute as they please so
that intensity of preference can be discerned, the use of
a lottery to prevent agenda manipulation.   These can all
serve as correctives to a crude operation of a majority
voting system.   There may well be others too.

Bruce Ackerman advances a more radical proposal.   He
suggests the possibility of a lottery in place of a majority vote (Ackerman, 1980, p. 288).   Where there are conflicting policies all of them go into a black box and the
one drawn out is implemented.   In the more familiar
device of majority voting the judgments of voters are
'added up' whilst in the lottery every voter has a finite
chance of deciding the political outcome.   In this respect the lottery recognizes the individual's autonomy and
also enshrines an equality amongst all voters.   On the
face of it it should be more appealing to democrats as a
mode of decision-making than majority voting.   Indeed it
may be so to some people.   But others may judge that majority voting, with all its flaws, has more to commend it.
Unlike the lottery it at least always pleases more people
than it displeases.   This is perhaps a feature which
should not be lightly disregarded.   As Ackerman points
out, however, finally to decide between these two modes of
decision-making we perhaps need more research.

Some people may have missed in this section a special
discussion of the 'permanent minority' and proposed solutions to that problem. (4)   It seems to me, however, that
the general devices I have suggested for modifying the
majority principle are sufficient to cope with the problems of respecting the autonomy of an entrenched (e.g.
religious) minority within the society.   It is important
to bear in mind that their basic civil rights are consti-
tutionally protected and also that in the democratic
society we are considering many decisions are made at
local, regional or work-place level.   There should therefore be considerable space for such minorities to live out
their particular life-style.   Finally there is the safeguard of the overview by the national forum of those cases
where a particular viewpoint, which does not violate any
constitutional rights, is persistently overridden over a
number of years.   These arrangements taken together would

seem to cover the problems raised for democracy by permanent minorities.

Several times in this section I have referred to the
need for political education to encourage people to consider the questions provoked by majority voting. Information and discussion of the issues is clearly badly
needed. As we saw at several points machinery, however
sophisticated, cannot replace an understanding of the
problems. In Chapter three we will look at the role of
political education in providing the kind of understanding
required.

DIRTY HANDS AND OPEN GOVERNMENT

We have discussed at a general level the kinds of institutions and machinery which might realize the principles
underlying a participatory democracy: the structure of
councils to allow for grassroots participation in decision-making; the national forum to monitor decisions in
the light of the constitutional framework of rights; provision for participation in decision-making at the work-
place; and the kind of modified form of the majority
principle which might be used when there is no consensus
on a policy or set of policies. Before we move on to
look at the educational institutions required in such a
society, we need to consider three topics all of importance for political education, which have not been covered
by the institutional framework so far outlined. First is
what I shall call for short the problem of 'dirty hands'.
More precisely, the issue I want to consider is whether
anyone involved in politics, particularly any office-
holder, will have, on occasion, to do something morally
reprehensible to forward some important and worthy political project. Bernard Williams, for instance, clearly
thinks that such office-holders will have to dirty their
hands:

> it is a predictable and probable hazard of public life
> that there will be these situations in which something
> morally disagreeable is clearly required. To refuse
> on moral grounds ever to do anything of that sort is
> more than likely to mean that one cannot seriously
> pursue even the moral ends of politics (Williams, 1978,
> p. 62).

It is clear from the paper that Williams has a number of
morally unacceptable acts and omissions in mind, including

'lying, or at least concealment and the making of misleading statements' (1978, p. 59).   Although Williams does
not give any concrete examples, two examples which might
fit the bill are provided by Sissela Bok in <u>Lying: Moral
Choice in Public and Private Life</u>.   She refers to two
similar cases of deception in presidential election campaigns (Bok, 1978, Chapter XII).   First, Roosevelt,
whilst moving the USA closer to entry into World War II,
was making statements like the following in his 1940 campaign to be re-elected: 'I have said this before, but I
shall say it again and again and again: Your boys are not
going to be sent into any foreign wars' (quoted in Bok,
1978, p. 179).   Similarly Lyndon Johnson in 1964, whilst
professing himself to be the candidate of peace, was preparing to escalate the war in Vietnam should he be re-
elected.

Since Williams does not consider these examples I do
not know whether he would think that in these cases the
deception of the electorate was a necessary, and therefore
justifiable, part of politics.   It seems to me, however,
that it is clearly not and that in a participatory democracy it would have no place.   If this reasoning is correct, this would provide further grounds for preferring
participatory democracy to other kinds.   Let us consider
why Roosevelt and Johnson might have felt themselves to be
justified in concealing their true policies from the electorate.   Presumably both of them were working with some
Schumpeter-like conception of themselves as rulers who
were chosen by competition to make policy decisions on
behalf of the electorate before presenting themselves
again for re-election.   Within this conception the electorate of course is seen as, by and large, politically incompetent.   This being so, benevolent rulers will often
face a problem.   On the one hand they will have formed a
view of what they see as the wisest policy which any responsible statesman should follow, while on the other, they
may well judge that the electorate, lacking access to all
the available information and, for this and other reasons,
being unable to make an informed political judgment, will
not share their view of the best policy.   This will have
the disastrous consequence that the 'right man' (i.e.,
Roosevelt or Johnson) with the political will to carry
through the 'right policies' will not be elected.   Assuming that Roosevelt and Johnson were not resorting to
deception simply to stay in power for some selfish end,
then something like the foregoing is the only kind of justification that either could advance for his campaign.
Given certain assumptions it is the <u>best</u> defence for

deceiving the electorate about the policies each would
pursue if elected.

   Is it necessary, however, to make 'certain assumptions'?   The participatory conception of democracy does
not.   It is based on the assumption, not that individual
citizens are politically incompetent, but that they are
responsible moral agents and should, as far as possible,
be involved in the making of political decisions themselves rather than have them made for them.   There is no
conception of 'consent' to a political elite who are en-
trusted with political power to make the 'right' decisions
and thus shoulder what might be considered to be impossible moral burdens for the ordinary citizen.   In so far,
therefore, as in any participatory democracy there is any
system of representatives (as there certainly would be in
the case of the national forum and in other contexts too),
then those representatives must be expected to place
before the electors honest accounts of the policies they
would pursue if elected.   Any concealment of policies
means that citizens are not able to vote according to the
candidates' policies and this is necessarily destructive
of the democratic system.   It is impossible to make a
rational choice amongst possible representatives and subsequently hold them to account for their performance in
office if one does not know what their policies will be.
This defence of deception as ultimately in the citizens'
best interests cannot, therefore, be reconciled with the
fundamental rationale for a participatory democracy.   Put
the other way round, participatory democracy rules out
such deception and should on that account be preferred to
the Schumpeter-type conception.   It might be argued that
this claim assumes that honesty must always be treated as
an absolute value.   On some occasions, however, perhaps
deception should be permitted in order that some greater
good may be realized.   This may well be the case in some
few circumstances and I shall try to deal with those
below.   To allow, however, that it applies in this case
is to make a whole range of assumptions, for instance
about the existence of political elites and politically
incompetent masses, which would run quite counter to all
the arguments for self-determination and against paternalism which were presented earlier in arguing the case for
participatory democracy.   These arguments would suggest
that it is not possible to justify political arrangements
which rest on systematic and carefully planned deception
of citizens by rulers.

What about those cases, however, where some minor

deception of citizens by rulers will secure some greater
good?   There must surely be a place for white lies in an
emergency and so even in a participatory democracy it
seems that politicians will have to dirty their hands.
Cases which might be thought to count as acceptable deceptions might include, for instance, those where the government denies that it is going to devalue (when in fact it
is) so as to avoid unfair profits to speculators, and
those where a 'cover story' is issued to the press to the
effect that it is a cold which is forcing a President to
return to the White House when in fact it is an international crisis.

There is a temptation to think that these are innocent
lies which are easily justifiable and that it would be
almost over-scrupulous to hold government spokesmen to
account for them.   As Sissela Bok points out (Bok, 1978,
pp. 170-81) however, by allowing such deceptions it is all
too easy for lying to become all-pervasive as a practice
in government.   Almost any lie can come to be justified
for the eventual greater good of the people and lies can
come to be used to keep the 'right people' (the honest,
upright politicians!) in power, to cover up past mistakes
or simply to sustain the present administration.   Lying
is an insidious practice.   It spreads and it is habit-
forming: those involved in it gradually become insensitive to considerations of veracity.   Sissela Bok elo-
quently describes this process.

For all Sissela Bok's eloquence and the stern moral
demands for honesty echoed here, will not the participatory democracy still have to countenance white lies in a
crisis like the ones mentioned?   Where devaluation is
concerned, it is not at all clear that it must, since a
firm policy of 'no comment' for such situations can be
established.   To be workable, however, this policy itself
must be strictly and honestly adhered to so that no comment means what it says and is not simply used when the
government does not want to admit that it is about to
devalue.   The 'cover story' case is harder to deal with.
First, without knowing a good deal more about the context
of this particular deception, it is hard to decide whether
it is justifiable or whether it falls into the same category as the Roosevelt or Johnson deceptions.   If the
thought behind the deceptive cover story is that if 'the
people' know the truth they will panic and this will have
all kinds of unhappy consequences, then this again rests
on a view of 'the people' which is incompatible with the
assumption behind a participatory democracy.   Let us sup-

pose, however, that some more substantial defence can be
put up for the cover story.   Perhaps for instance it is
essential if international tension is not to be increased.
If we further suppose that such a case cannot be covered
by a policy agreed to in advance by citizens, we may have
an example of an excusable deception.   Who is to judge,
however, whether it is an excusable deception?   Only in
my view the citizens with hindsight.   Any government or
member of a government which has practised such deception
must subsequently offer to resign and stand for re-election.   This is, I think, the only way that one can ensure
that governments are accountable for their deceptive practices.   Failure to comply with this procedure would have
to attract the heaviest penalty, for instance individuals'
being debarred from holding public office again.

The rationale of and basic assumptions underlying par
ticipatory democracy rule out, or put considerable curbs
on, a great number of the deceptions which politicians
feel justified in employing within a representative democracy like our own.   What are seen as permissible deceptions from the standpoint of rulers conceived of as a
benevolent and wise political elite taking care of the
interests of their subjects are ruled out by an egalitarian stance towards the exercise of political power which
assumes that, as far as possible, power must be shared
amongst morally responsible and morally competent citizens.   Ruled out too, and for the same reasons, is unnecessary secrecy on the part of government.   British
government, whatever party is in power, is notoriously the
least open of the democratic governments with which we are
familiar.   In fact if a British citizen wanted to have
information about all kinds of things which she might well
think she had a right to know - from, for instance, the
hygiene and safety standards in British cooked meat pro-
cessing plants and details of defective British bicycles
and motor vehicles, to plans for the evacuation of areas
around nuclear plants in the case of accidents - she would
need to get such information from US government files, as
British researchers do (Michael, 1982, Chapter one).   In
Britain the relevant reports are secret and unavailable;
in the USA, under the Freedom of Information Act, they are
open to inspection.   I do not want to go into details
about the boundary between necessary and unnecessary
secrecy in government, since this would take us too far
from the main issues of the institutions and machinery for
democratic government with which this chapter is concerned.   It will be clear that, as with deception, the
presumption must be in favour of openness and the free

availability of information to citizens, since only in
these conditions can they take decisions or assess the
wisdom of decisions taken by others on their behalf.
Openness must be the rule except in those cases where it
would lead to considerable harm being done to quite innocent communities or individuals.   Certainly whatever
policy is finally adopted must be the result of open
debate and discussion on the issue of what is and what is
not to be secret and confidential.

In this treatment of the topic of 'dirty hands' I have
concentrated on the deception which might be thought to be
justifiable on some views of democracy and so built into
the democratic arrangements.   It is expected that election campaigners like Roosevelt and Johnson will not be
telling the whole truth but presenting their respective
cases in the best possible light, which may well involve
omitting some facts or considerations.   I have concentrated on this kind of deception and the related topic of
secrecy by governments because, as I have tried to show,
these undesirable practices, whilst ruled in on some conceptions of democracy, are firmly ruled out on a participatory view.   I have not considered practices, like the
accepting of bribes, which would be ruled out on any view
of democracy.   I have also not yet examined the problem
Thomas Nagel raises in 'Ruthlessness in Public Life'
(Nagel, 1978).   Here Nagel is concerned not with deception but with another claim made about political systems,
namely that the use of coercion and manipulative methods
is permissible in the public sphere when they would not be
in private life.   Nagel gives two examples, conscription
and taxation.   Of taxation he says:

> If someone with an income of $2,000 a year trains a gun
> on someone with an income of $100,000 a year and makes
> him hand over his wallet, that is robbery.   If the
> federal government witholds a portion of the second
> person's salary (enforcing the laws against tax evasion
> with threats of imprisonment under armed guard) and
> gives some of it to the first person in the form of
> welfare payments, food stamps, or free health care,
> that is taxation.   In the first case it is (in my
> opinion) an impermissible use of coercive means to
> achieve a worthwhile end.   In the second case the
> means are legitimate, because they are impersonally
> imposed by an institution designed to promote certain
> results (Nagel, 1978, p. 88).

In Nagel's view it is not because of the citizens' consent
to it that taxation is legitimate:

> Consent is not needed to justify such legislative
> action, because the legislature is an institution whose
> authority to make such decisions on consequentialist
> grounds is morally justified in other ways.   Its
> periodic answerability to the electorate is one feature
> of the institution (another being the constitutional
> protection of rights) that contributes to its legiti-
> macy - but not by implying each citizen's consent to
> its actions (Nagel, 1978, p. 87).

I find Nagel's views puzzling.   It seems to me that consent does enter into the justification of taxation.
There has to be consent on the part of citizens to a
system of taxation (of whatever kind) and to a body, or
set of bodies, which will determine actual taxation policy,
if the moral autonomy of citizens is to be equally respec-
ted.   It may be that Nagel would allow such consent to
the whole system and that what he is denying is that a
particular taxation policy is legitimate, if, and only if,
every citizen has consented to it.   If we assume that
that is what he intends, this particular problem of ruthlessness in politics is clearly different from the issues
of deception and secrecy discussed already and it will be
clear why I have separated it off from those.   The problem in the taxation (and perhaps the conscription)
case (5) arises with those citizens who do not support the
policy and are therefore coerced into conforming with it.
This however is the problem discussed in the previous section, the problem of the minority which cannot agree with
the majority decision.   To label it in this way is not of
course to dismiss it, for it is perhaps the most intractable problem for democratic theory, particularly on a participatory view of democracy which lays stress on the conception of the citizen as a responsible moral agent.   It
is, however, to suggest that since it is a different problem, it cannot like the cases of deception be almost entirely eliminated from democracy (on the participatory
view of democracy):   a whole variety of means will have to
be considered to modify the operation of the majority
principle to take account of it.   This was suggested in
the previous section and will be considered again in the
discussion of civil disobedience.

The participatory democracy, then, in its basic
rationale and procedures is antithetical to deception,
even benevolent deception, and to secrecy.   It also

recognizes the problem of the coercion and manipulation of
the minority and must, given its rationale, be committed
to a search for practices and procedures (e.g. devolution
of decision-making, the device of the quantum of votes,
etc.: see previous section) to mitigate the operation of
the majority principle.   Other things being equal, this
provides further grounds for preferring this form of democracy over others.

FRATERNITY

In Chapter one certain basic attributes of the democratic
citizen were discussed, but since at that point the conception of the participatory democracy had not been outlined a complete treatment of the kind of attitudes which
citizens in such a society should have towards each other
had to be delayed.   Among the points about attitudes that
were made in Chapter one, it was stated that in any democratic society individuals must be tolerant of others involved in very different activities and styles of life.
This is a delineation of an essentially stand-off relationship.   It is necessary but not sufficient in a participatory democracy, for its citizens must also stand in a
fraternal relationship to each other.   What does this
mean?   What is demanded over and above the tolerance referred to, if people are to have fraternal attitudes to
their fellow-citizens?

    Perhaps this attitude is best delineated by contrast
with a number of others which are similar to it, or con-
tingently connected with it but distinct from it.   A simplistic approach to fraternity regards it as the attitude
which necessarily obtains between those involved in a communal project.   The rough idea here is that if people are
putting up tents together, or playing in orchestras, feelings of comradeship and togetherness will be generated.
There are two points to note.   First, engagements in communal projects may not generate such feelings, but feelings of competitiveness, envy, even hostility.   Second,
even if they do generate more positive feelings of, for
instance, liking to be in the company of others, such
feelings may not be sufficient or even necessary, for the
fraternal attitude.   This will become clear, I think, as
we probe this and related attitudes further.

    Suppose we consider people engaged in co-operative ven-
tures.   Here, it might be thought, if people actually
want to co-operate with others in some joint leisure

activity like sailing a boat or in some business enterprise, this involves their being willing to fit in with
others, to do their share, to display, in other words, co-
operative attitudes. And if one has such attitudes, is
this not just another way of saying that one stands in a
fraternal relationship with the others involved? After
all such a person need not see her colleagues simply as
functionaries to be judged only in terms of their contribution to the venture. It is quite compatible with this
view for her to regard them also as people with lives outside the enterprise and with their own interests, projects, hopes, fears and worries. Yet, I want to claim,
this need not be a fraternal relationship. What is lacking, then? Why should one want to resist the idea that
these people stand in a fraternal relationship to one
another?

Some have suggested that it is affection or liking
which is missing. These are difficult notions in an area
where one needs to make a number of fine distinctions,
because the feelings and emotions here range from those of
sexual attraction, to a kind of aesthetic delight in the
configuration of features found in another person, to a
pleasure in the company of someone sharing similar values
to oneself, or perhaps radically different ones. For
this reason it is easy to say very silly things about
liking and friendship, as even Aristotle does. I shall
try to avoid that by not making any attempt at a full-
scale examination of these notions. Instead I shall
simply try to state what I think people may have in mind
when they suggest that something like liking is the element required. This is that liking someone involves,
among other things, enjoying that person's company and
wanting, other things being equal, to spend more time in
it. Even if, however, the members of the co-operative
group enjoy one another's company, they may do so in the
way that a nephew might enjoy the company of four eccen-
tric aunts. They are fun to be with, they are all really
rather 'cards'. One may have those feelings, and they
are quite common in groups which have worked together over
time and whose members have come to appreciate each
others' foibles and eccentricities, but one may still not
feel fraternal to one's aunts or workmates. What, then,
is the elusive missing element? It seems to be the feeling of a bond between oneself and other as equals. To
feel fraternal towards others is basically to relate to
them as equals. That is why the co-operative group whose
members see one another not simply as co-operators but
also as people with lives outside the enterprise is not

necessarily a fraternal one, because the members may not
perceive any common bonds relating them as equals.   It is
common, for instance, to find employers who appreciate
their employees as good members of the workforce (as good
co-operators) and who realize that they have lives outside
the plant (they have hobbies like angling and take holidays in Margate) but who feel no common bonds with them as
equals.   Indeed they may feel that their own attitudes to
life, the whole pattern of their sensibilities and sympathies set them in a world apart from their employees.

   As we noted, liking one's colleagues is not a sufficient condition of having fraternal attitudes towards
them.   Is it even necessary?   In the sense in which I
have taken it, as enjoying people's company and wanting to
spend time with them, it seems not to be.   If something
like this is right, why do I claim that citizens in a participatory democracy must feel fraternal towards each
other?   If they are tolerant of others with different
styles of life and so on, as suggested earlier and in
Chapter one, why do they need, in addition, to stand in a
fraternal relationship?   Fraternity as I have outlined
it, namely as feeling a bond between oneself and others as
equals, as moral beings with the same basic needs and an
interest in leading a life of one's own, is the necessary
emotional attitude between citizens who hold that one of
the basic principles of their society is that power must
be exercised, or controlled, equally by all moral agents
who form the citizen body.   It is the only appropriate
attitude for one citizen to have towards another.   Servility on the one hand, or patronage on the other, or any
related attitudes on the continuum in between, must be
ruled out by the basic values underpinning the participatory democracy.   Fraternity is the attitude which accom-
panies the principles outlined in Chapter one and serves
as the dynamic motivating force behind the setting up of
the institutions designed to implement those principles
and in their subsequent operation.

   This is clear if we recollect our earlier discussion of
the majority principle.   At the end of that discussion we
were left with the nagging problem of the minority, a
worse problem if it is a permanent minority, but always
bad.   It was suggested that there is a need to try and
find new machinery which will cope with the problems of
conflicts over policies in a way which more perfectly
realizes the underlying principles of the participatory
democracy.   Meanwhile it was argued that citizens have a
duty to mitigate the worst effects of majority voting on

the wants and interests of minorities by, for instance,
striving to reach compromises or in some situations devol-
ving decision-making so that minorities in the whole community become majorities in some local decision-making
body.   To undertake the search for new machinery or to
attempt to mitigate the effects of current decision-making
procedures on minorities, citizens have to want to make
the whole situation a more equal one.   They will want to
do these things, other things being equal, if they feel
themselves to be related to their fellows in the community
as equals.   If I strongly feel myself linked by fraternal
bonds to others in my community I shall want not to profit
at their expense, but want their interests and projects to
flourish along with my own.   Exactly the same point can
be made in relation to the cases of deception and secrecy
discussed in the section on dirty hands.   If one feels
oneself to be in a community of equals, one will not want
to practise the deception or secrecy considered there
because both the selfish desire to maintain oneself in a
position of power and the paternalistic desire to protect
weaker brethren from their follies are not motives compatible with such a feeling.   Fraternity amongst the citizen
body is the vital motivating force if the machinery
through which the democratic principles are implemented is
to be constructed and used in the right spirit.

This account of participatory democracy puts considerable weight on the necessary role played by fraternity.
Critics may suggest that this is where the whole project
must founder because such feelings, whilst strong in some
individuals, do not occur naturally in all of us.   Some
may even wish to oppose the development of such feelings,
even if it were possible.   As Donald MacRae says:

> The doctrine of alienation is related to the most dan-
> gerous and least rewarding aspect of the French revolu-
> tion: the terrifying injunction to fraternity.   To
> speak very personally and seriously, I approve both
> liberty and equality;   I regard it as an essential
> liberty that I am not promiscuously called 'Brother'.
> I welcome the division of labour and the diversity,
> even the anomie of advanced society (MacRae, 1969, p.
> 69).

Let us take the point about the naturalness of such feelings first.   In this respect the feelings of fraternity I
have talked about are no different from, say, feelings of
sympathy or gratitude or indignation.   All of these are
learned.   There seems to be no reason why people should

not learn to feel fraternal.   This will involve acquiring
both certain beliefs about one's fellow-citizens and also
a certain attitude towards them.   It should not be impossible for education, broadly conceived, to do something
about both aspects.   We cannot at the moment dismiss that
possibility.   We cannot regard the fact that children do
not at present develop into fraternal citizens as a failure of education to achieve an aim to which it is seriously bending enormous effort and energy, since in the communities with which we are familiar the promotion of fraternity is not a significant educational aim.   We should
also note that in a fully-fledged participatory democracy
fraternal attitudes will both underpin the institutions of
the society and also be themselves undergirded by the
social structure which does not permit gross discrepancies
in the share of primary goods between citizens.   This
will minimize the structural obstacles in the way of citizens relating to each other as equals.   In our society,
although it is possible for individuals to relate to
others as moral beings with the same basic needs and an
interest in leading a life of their own, it is made harder
rather than easier by a structure which, for instance,
permits some an income ten times that of others.   The
participatory democracy can turn what can be a vicious
circle in our society into a benign one;   it can encourage
individuals to relate to each other as equals so that they
want, for this reason, to ensure that intstitutions secure
to all their fair shares.

    In Chapter three we will be examining a political edu-
cation in which the promotion of fraternity is a prominent
aim.   We can consider there the strategies suggested to
achieve it and their likely success.   Certainly there
seem to be no a priori grounds for pessimism about the
possibility of people coming to acquire fraternal attitudes.

    Even if it is possible to develop fraternal attitudes,
however, should we do so?   MacRae's outspoken rejection
of the ideal is echoed by many of those working in the
liberal democratic tradition.   But is MacRae attacking
the ideal of fraternity I have been developing here?   He
seems concerned that if he embraces fraternity he will be
committed to uniformity in life-styles and to an unlooked-
for 'togetherness'.   But as I was careful to argue, the
notion of fraternity employed here goes along with a tolerance of diversity in others' life-styles and interests
and carries no demands that people should engage in communal projects or should enjoy spending the major part of
their time in the company of their fellows.

This account has attempted to separate fraternity from
apparently related ideas.   I have tried to argue that a
fraternal attitude, necessarily connected with the principle of justice underpinning the democratic state, must
be encouraged in all citizens.

CIVIL DISOBEDIENCE

In Chapter one we examined the principles underlying participatory democracy and in this chapter we have considered the institutions and arrangements for decision-making
which might realize those principles.   We have ruled out
certain practices inimical to the working of democratic
institutions and we have explored the attitude citizens
should have towards their fellows if the institutions are
to work well.   If the institutions, arrangements and
attitudes all worked perfectly according to this rationale
there would be no need for this present section.   Even a
society, however, which conscientiously tried to organize
itself in every detail according to this plan could not
expect perfection.   We have to face the possibility of
mistakes, negligence, selfishness, authoritarian attitudes,
all interfering with the working of the democratic institutions.   Most of the errors and anti-democratic attitudes and their consequences will be taken care of by the
inbuilt procedures of accountability in the democratic
system and any wrongs redressed.

There are cases, however, which the accountability
machinery will not pick up.   One such is the minority
which strongly objects to the majority decision but can do
nothing about it within the framework of the decision-
making process.   We can imagine, for instance, the majority agreeing to fight what the minority considers to be an
injust war.   The minority tries all the legitimate methods usually used to get a political body to change its
mind.   Letters and articles putting the opposing case
appear in the newspapers, spokesmen of the minority appear
on television, informal lobbying goes on, there are even
large peaceful protests, marches and rallies.   But the
majority stands firmly by its decision.   What can the
minority do?   They might simply accept the decision,
holding it to be foolish and even morally wrong, but going
along with it.   But if this is too much for their con-
sciences to bear there remains the possibility of civil
disobedience.

Let me make clear what I understand by civil disobed-

ience.   An act of civil disobedience is similar to a
crime in that it involves the breaking of a law, but there
the resemblance ends.   In the case of civil disobedience
the law will be a minor, or unimportant one, say, a
traffic or parking regulation, but one where its infringement, especially by large numbers of people, is likely to
cause considerable disruption.   The law will be broken
not for some personal objective of a worthy or unworthy
kind - for instance stealing a loaf of bread to feed
starving children or a jar of caviar from Harrods to
impress one's friends - but for a political objective.
The objective will usually be to draw attention to an act
or omission on the part of a political body which is held
to be a grave injustice and/or seriously harmful to the
interests of a segment of the population.   Acts of civil
disobedience are not violent acts, where the intention is
to threaten or use violence.   If they were, they would be
acts of political violence or terrorism.   The intention
behind an act of civil disobedience is to draw attention
to a political grievance in a dramatic way.   It is rather
like a protest march, but goes beyond the protest march in
causing inconvenience and disruption, often to the participants themselves as well.   Traffic obstruction, for
instance, not only disrupts the flow of traffic, but may
well clog the courts with hearings of many hundreds of
minor offences, as well as causing the participants to be
fined.

The above account gives a rough and ready picture of
civil disobedience and marks it off reasonably well from
political terrorism.   There are further points one could
attempt to settle - for instance, is willingness to suffer
punishment a criterion of civil disobedience? - and there
is a considerable literature through which this and other
issues could be pursued;   but for our immediate purposes
these can be left on one side. (6)   Our immediate task is
to see if civil disobedience can be justified and for that
the present account will suffice.   I should add at this
point that I am not discussing political violence and acts
of terrorism which, unlike acts of civil disobedience, may
have as part of the intention behind them that fellow-
citizens be injured or killed.   In a participatory democracy these could never be justifiable.   Recall that we
are not concerned with a political body bent on policies
of oppression but with one which seeks to further citizens' interests but which, operated as it is by human
beings, may be adversely affected by mistakes, negligence,
cover-ups, authoritarian attitudes.   In certain regimes
it may be possible under certain conditions to justify

carefully specified types of political violence (see
Honderich, 1980, Chapters four and five).   It is hard to
see how this could ever be justifiable in a participatory
democracy.   In so far as anyone might judge that political violence was necessary, it seems clear that the
society would have moved far away from the participatory
ideal and would thus be outside the scope of this essay.

Given that we are concerned only with civil disobedience, under what circumstances would it be justified?
One might be tempted to think that it would be ruled out
as firmly as political violence.   There could after all
be a great number of official and permitted activities,
protest marches, demonstrations and so on, so could people
ever be justified in breaking the law to achieve a political objective?   I want to argue that they might be but
that they would need to acquire political judgment through
political education enabling them to see whether or not
they would be justified on any particular occasion.   This
is because in any particular case a number of factors need
to be weighed against each other.   Judgment is necessary
first of all to determine (i) whether or not the political
objective is sufficiently important to merit the likely
disruption the law-breaking will cause.   Extreme cases
present few problems.   Clearly the civil rights issues
and the anti-Vietnam war campaign in the USA in the 1960s
and early 1970s were important enough.   If a local council wanted to change the colour of the litter bins this
would almost certainly not be.   There are likely to be
many cases between these extremes where the individual
will be considerably exercised over whether or not her
political objective is sufficiently important to merit
illegal action.   Political education, although it cannot
provide a slide rule to measure the importance of political objectives, can at least prepare the individual to
face such judgments.   Importance must, in any case, be
considered alongside the question (ii) whether or not the
political authority concerned is or is not going to do
anything about the issue.   The objective might be an
important one, but if it seems likely that the government
is going to take action over it in the very near future
civil disobedience may be an unnecessary indulgence.
Finally (iii) the means chosen to draw attention to the
grievances must be as limited as is compatible with their
achieving the objective, which is to get authorities to
reconsider their policies.

Even if, however, all three conditions are satisfied,
there may still remain doubts about whether civil disobed-

ience is ever justifiable in a participatory democracy.
Would this perhaps be tantamount to political blackmail?
I am not sure if civil disobedience is correctly described
as political blackmail, but I am certainly suggesting that
in some instances a limited illegal use of power is justifiable.   In the particular instance with which we began,
that of an implacable majority exercising power over a
minority, those indulging in civil disobedience are using
a limited amount of power to bring home to the majority
that there are people who take a different moral view of
the situation.   The majority are being asked, fairly for-
cibly, to reconsider their views.   In this respect civil
disobedience may be said to even up somewhat the power relationship between the majority and the minority.   In
certain circumstances, as where the minority is faced with
a policy to fight what it considers to be an unjust war,
individuals may judge that a limited illegal use of power
is justifiable.

It will be important in political education programmes
to bring home to people that besides their political
duties of participation and so on they may, on some occasions, have a duty to be civilly disobedient.   When and
how will often be difficult to determine but historical
cases of civil disobedience may help one to judge.   Were
the suffragettes, the anti-Vietnam war campaigners justified in civil disobedience viewed from the perspective
available to them at the time?   The whole topic will need
careful treatment in a political education programme -
pupils should, for instance, be disabused of the idea that
civil disobedience is the only option if a vote goes
against one - but it is not a topic that should be avoided.
It can obviously profitably be linked with work on decision-making and majority voting.

STRATEGIES

In the course of Chapter one and this one I have elaborated the basic principles of democracy and discussed in
some detail their implementation within the institutions
of a fully democratic society - or at least a society as
democratic as human frailty will allow.   That setting is
not, however, the democratic society in which any contemporary readers will find themselves.   How then should I
proceed from here?

After setting out the arrangements for the provision
and control of education in a participatory democracy, I

could just stop and let these thoughts stand as a suggested blue-print for a future democratic society, to be discussed, approved or rejected by any interested readers.
I am not, however, inclined to do that. I want rather to
move on and talk about strategies and policies for changing from the kind of constitutional democracies (7) we are
familiar with to the participatory democracy outlined.
It seems to me that there are better and worse ways of
moving from our present situation to a participatory democracy and these can be publicly debated. The rest of
this book can be seen as a contribution to such a debate.
At this point some readers may feel uneasy. Whilst they
may have been reasonably happy to follow the case presented thus far for the basic principles and institutions,
they may wonder what kind of credentials I can present to
justify adopting certain policies rather than others to
bring about the desired participatory arrangements. It
might be thought that these policies about ways and means
are matters for empirical investigation by political sci-
entists rather than a philosopher. To some extent this
is true, of course. At a number of points we shall have
to leave some aspects of certain policies to be settled
when the outcome of empirical investigation is known.
There are, however, points for the philosopher, too, to
make about acceptable strategies. First, certain policies can be shown to involve inconsistencies: some, for
instance, may presuppose an encouragement of competitiveness amongst citizens which would fit ill with the democratic society they are endeavouring to realize. Identifying such unacceptable policies is clearly a philosophical task and there are many worthy examples in political philosophy of philosophers at work in this way. (8)
Second, given her reflection on the principles involved,
there is no reason, it seems to me, why the philosopher
should be debarred from suggesting policies which might
realize these principles - given always that further empirical work may be required to see if these suggestions
are worth entertaining.

In the following three chapters I shall be talking
about one aspect of education, namely political education,
and two social roles, those of parents and headteachers,
which will be very different in the participatory democracy from the forms in which we know them in contemporary
society, and I shall be suggesting policies which might
bring about those changes. Given the educational focus
of this essay the pivotal role of political education in
this process of change will be apparent. The next chapter deals with this. Parents and headteachers are less

obvious cases for treatment.   However, for anyone interested in an advance towards participatory democracy, the
rights and responsibilities traditionally associated with
these roles require careful examination and revision.
Interestingly both roles often seem to cause their contemporary occupants much trouble and heartsearching.   This
attempt at a reassessment of them is perhaps timely.

Political education   *3*

This chapter begins with a discussion of the control and
provision of education in general in a participatory democracy. As we shall see the issues raised bear closely on
the topic of political education, the nature of which in a
participatory democracy is discussed in section two.   A
third section is devoted to some philosophical considerations relating to the form political education should take
now in our society.   The chapter ends with two policy
recommendations.

THE CONTROL OF EDUCATION

In talking about education in this essay I am, for the
most part, confining myself to the basic formal education
provided for young people, e.g. that provided in schools
in our own society for pupils from five to sixteen.   In
some future work I would like to talk about the democratic
society's policies towards higher education, professional
trainings of all types, the provision of opportunities for
learning activities outside the education system, and the
potentially educative effects of social institutions and
the media.   Here I shall only gesture towards some of
those areas whilst concentrating on the provision and control of basic education.

   It might seem that we already know who is to determine
what this basic education should consist in and how it
should be organized.   In the previous chapter the point
was made that work-places, like other organizations, must
be subject to democratic organization and control.
Schools, like factories or hospitals, are work-places, so
it would seem to follow that what is provided in any particular school will be a matter of what its work-force

decides to offer, subject only to any general guidelines
laid down by the national forum (see Chapter two, p. 39f).
Formally speaking this is correct, but there is an important difference between factories and schools in the way
in which each is affected by the national guidelines.
For the most part a factory is likely to be only lightly
regulated.   The role of the national guidelines is to
protect constitutional rights (to outlaw, for instance,
practices which discriminate against ethnic groups) and to
ensure that policies which favour sectional groups are not
pursued at the expense of the public interest (see, for
instance, in Chapter two the example of the transport
policy, pp. 46-7). Within these boundaries individuals are
free to set up enterprises to produce whatever they please
from elastic bands to machine tools.

On schools, however, the national guidelines will bear
more heavily.   Their role is still, of course, to protect
constitutional rights and ensure that the policies of
individual organizations do not run counter to the public
interest.   The difference is that the school is in business to provide people with a primary good, namely education, which is one of their constitutional rights (see
Chapter one, p. 11).   As I have argued elsewhere, in a
democratic society it is in the individual's interest and
the public interest that she has an education which enables her to participate in society as a responsible citizen (White, P., 1973).   That means an education which en-
courages her to develop autonomously, to be able to distinguish what is in her real interests from what she may
currently want, or have been brought to want and enables
her to understand and participate in the exercise and control of power.   The provision of such an education as a
primary good, itself a means to further primary goods, is
the whole raison d'être of educational institutions and
thus their activities must be subject to considerable control by the national guidelines.

Some people may accept that there should be political
control over education but question why it should come
from the centre.   Why national guidelines?   Why not
devolve educational decisions down to local groups and let
each locality or community interpret the constitutional
right to education as it sees fit?   Against such total
devolution, it seems to me, there are no moral arguments
but there are practical and political ones.   The practical ones need not detain us.   They are concerned with,
for instance, the desirability of a certain uniformity of
learning objectives and school organization so that the

training of teachers and also the transfer of teachers and
pupils between different educational institutions in different parts of the country is facilitated.   The political arguments concern the most appropriate machinery for
guaranteeing the constitutional right to education for all
citizens and ensuring that educational policies are in the
public interest.   As we saw in Chapter two, this monitor-
ing/co-ordinating role has to be performed by some accountable authority standing <u>outside</u> the network of local
groups.   We introduced there the institution of the
national forum.   This body is required just as much in
the educational sphere as in the industrial one.

The details of the division of labour between the
national forum and the schools and teachers in any locality will be for any participatory democracy to decide in
its historical situation.   But it is possible to make
three general points about how the guidelines will bear on
schools. (1)

(i)   One aspect of the individual's constitutional right
to education concerns her entitlement to an education
which will enable her to become a responsible citizen,
able to exercise and control power.   Either to exercise
power herself or to hold other wielders of power accountable she will need certain necessary intellectual equip-
ment.   This will constitute the minimum we can demand of
citizens, even those who are not themselves directly involved in large-scale decision-making.   The process of
accountability is not a straightforward matter of the political bodies presenting their records to the individual
citizen for her discrete, individual consideration.   In
the participatory democracy there will be a complex machinery of accountability - checks within political bodies,
watchdog committees, comment from independent media like
newspapers and television - but ultimately, using these
resources, the individual, as a morally responsible
person, will have to arrive at her own assessment.   The
educational bedrock enabling her to do this is a broad
understanding in the main areas of knowledge.   Given the
institutional structure we are assuming, this means that
institutions providing basic education must ensure that
all their pupils enjoy a broad curriculum, including, for
instance, mathematics, the human and physical sciences,
history and the arts.   If political bodies are to be held
accountable, the citizen must be able to judge that they
have taken all relevant considerations into account in
arriving at their policies.   Even this fairly modest requirement will be impossible unless the citizen has some

awareness of the considerations which could bear on political decisions.   The extent to which tackling such political problems as pollution, conservation and population
control depends on a great range of different kinds of
knowledge is demonstrated in masterly fashion by John
Passmore in Man's Responsibility for Nature (Passmore,
1974).   It may well be that some of these considerations,
for instance mathematical ones, bear on political problems
more rarely than others, but with political problems, as
with moral ones, one cannot say in advance what knowledge
will bear on them and what not.   A broad general curriculum is thus the first requirement for citizens in a democracy if they are to act in a politically responsible
manner and the broad framework of this curriculum will be
laid down by the national forum.   Within this framework
individual localities and teachers in them will determine
the more particular selection of content in the light of
their own strengths and local conditions and opportunities.

As well as laying down the framework for the broad curriculum the national forum will have to ensure that explicit attention is given to political education, both (a) on
the theoretical side, enabling pupils, e.g., to develop
coherent frameworks of political concepts and also the
ability to assess political arguments which will involve
the acquisition of relevant factual political knowledge;
and, (b), on the dispositional side, so that pupils are
disposed to care about political matters. (2)   Again the
broad objectives will be nationally determined, whilst
working out the means to achieve them will be the task of
the local schools and teachers in them.

(ii)   As well as guidelines on the content of education -
the broad curriculum required and on political education
in particular - there will be general guidelines on teaching methods and the organization of educational institutions.   These are likely to take the negative form of,
for instance, ruling out indoctrination and certain kinds
of hierarchical authority structures, unnecessary secrecy,
and manipulative devices.   Within these boundaries members of each institution will be left to work out their
own teaching and organizational arrangements.

The case has already been made for content guidelines
if the child's constitutional right to exercise and control power is to be guaranteed.   Guidelines for teaching
and the organizational structure of the school are equally
necessary, not least since the child acquires a consider-

able amount of her political knowledge in an informal way
through her membership of the educational institution.
It would be foolish to have carefully worked out content
guidelines whilst leaving teaching procedures and particularly the structure of the school unregulated.

(iii) The guidelines elaborated under (i) and (ii) concern the individual's education as a democratic citizen,
although the broad curriculum provided for in (i) would
also obviously contribute to her more general development.
To foster her development as an autonomous person the
national forum would also need to lay down guidelines to
ensure that as wide as possible a range of activities and
learning experiences were available in any locality.
This would take the negative form of outlawing any restriction of activities and the positive one of using
sports and arts subsidies to help widen options for young
people beyond basic education.   An elaboration of this
argument will be found in Chapter five.   There I shall
argue that it is in large part the parents' responsibility
to guide their children towards such options, although it
is the community's responsibility to provide the resources
for them.

The preceding three points indicate the three broad
areas of the national guidelines.   The details of the
machinery for producing these, including that regulating
the relationship between the central body and the teachers
in any given locality, will need to be determined in the
historical situation in which people find themselves.

Some readers may think that while it is reasonable for
me to refuse to provide a detailed blue-print, they have
been told enough to feel considerably troubled about the
role of teachers in a participatory democracy.   Whatever
the details of the machinery turn out to be, teachers must
necessarily come out, they may argue, as a depressed
class.   They are the people who know about the process of
education but their professional judgments about, for
instance, the aims of education are to be overruled by a
political body, the national forum, whose behests they
must implement as mere functionaries.   Leaving aside the
highly coloured language of behests and functionaries I
make no bones about endorsing this as a correct expression
of the way things must be.   Teachers can be in no privileged position as regards the aims of education, since
these are necessarily connected with views on the good for
man and the good society.   They are not moral experts on
these matters any more than any other sectional group is

and they cannot be allowed to determine the community's
overall goals and policies, as they would be doing if the
control of education, including its aims, were solely in
their hands.   But this is not to say that teachers' professional judgments are to be discounted as they obedient-
ly carry out the tasks assigned by their political mas-
ters.   On curriculum and school organization the national
forum only lays down guidelines.   Within the broad framework for the curriculum it will be for teachers in individual schools, or localities, to decide on detailed syllabuses.   Here their professional judgment will come into
play as they decide in the light of their pupils' abilities and experience, local resources, their own strengths
and weaknesses, what particular topics they will cover and
in what way.   Similarly where school organization is concerned teachers, along with others working in the institution, will be able to establish their own internal
arrangements for the running of the school.   On the
detailed means to be employed in achieving educational
aims the teachers and educational theorists are authorities, able to deploy their educational judgments on appropriate programmes, sequences of topics, modes of teaching
and so on as completely autonomous professionals.

It is perhaps worth pointing out as a kind of aside
that there are certain modes of teaching and certain subjects which will be ruled out by the aims of education in
the participatory democracy.   As we saw in (ii) above,
any kind of indoctrination - that is getting people to
believe propositions unshakeably against all possible evidence - is not allowable.   The organizational guidelines
will explicitly rule out all forms of this.   A full-blown
case of indoctrination through the structure of educational institutions would be the intentional design of the
organization to induce in its members certain unshakeable
beliefs.   Clearly this would be antithetical to participatory democracy and fairly unlikely to occur.   What the
organizational guidelines are intended to prevent, however, is unintentional indoctrination via the structure of
educational institutions whereby, for instance, members
came to believe that they held an elite or lowly place
within the society.   Teachers are unlikely to find such
attempts to improve practice unduly irksome.

Certain subjects, too, will be ruled out, most notably
perhaps religion if taught as a faith to be accepted.
Religion as a social phenomenon considered sociologically,
historically and as a background to the various litera-
tures of the world will, of course, be studied in its

major forms.   What will not be permitted is conversion of
children into good Christians, Moslems, Hindus and so on.
This ·is because imparting and encouraging of particular
faiths runs counter to the basic aim of encouraging personal autonomy and allowing children to choose a way of
life.   What of parents' rights in this matter?   In Chapter five we will be looking at the parents' right to con-
vert their child into a good Christian, etc. outside the
basic education system.

   With such qualifications as these in respect of teaching methods and subjects ruled out by the basic principles
of the participatory democracy, teachers are free to
interpret national curriculum and organizational policies
as they see fit in their own contexts.   For them to
demand the right wholly to determine educational aims and
curricula would clearly be unjustifiable and would amount
to a claim to exercise more power over the future shape of
the society than any sectional group can be allowed.

   This then is a sketch of the broad structure for the
provision and control of basic education within a participatory democracy.   It provides a background for the sections more specifically on political education which
follow.

POLITICAL EDUCATION IN A PARTICIPATORY DEMOCRACY

Political education in the participatory democracy is not
conceived as an extra subject to be tacked on to the curriculum.   In this respect there is the strongest contrast
with our society in which in recent years there has been
considerable agitation about widespread political ignorance and apathy among young people and recommendations
have been made for beginning political education as a specific subject in the first school and introducing it into
the secondary school curriculum (see, e.g., Crick and
Porter, 1978; and Robins and Robins, 1978).   By contrast
in the participatory democracy people are politically educated through all the structures of the society and this
process is made explicit in basic education.

   Let us consider how this operates by looking first at
the education system.   What one needs to grasp here is
that political education provides the framework for the
whole of education.   It is not simply one element within
it, either tacked on or integrated: it is the context for
the whole enterprise.   At this point I need to dispel

obvious misinterpretations of what I am saying.   I am not
suggesting any such crude politicizing of the curriculum
and whole educational process as is often associated with
totalitarian regimes.   I am not suggesting, for instance,
only those literary texts with an explicitly political
aspect, like Brecht's Galileo or Trollope's novels, or
those parts of science which have some explicit bearing on
contemporary problems like pollution or population control, or political history concentrating narrowly on the
activities of parliaments and other ruling groups.   By
saying that the whole of education is set within a political framework I mean that the structure of the education
itself expresses a certain political stance.   The education has the structure it does because this is the way the
community thinks it can best realize the values and attitudes to which it is committed.   If a child within the
system asks why it takes the form it does - in basic education, in the particular organization of her school and
so on - the answer must come back in political terms.
The rationale for the basic education involves spelling
out the community's conception of the development of the
individual as an autonomous person and a citizen; detail-
ing the reasons for the range of optional activities young
people are encouraged to sample involves an elaboration of
the community's conception of the person and the pluralis-
tic society in which people can best be supported in
making the best of themselves; the rationale for the
particular organization of the school involves an account
of the form authority structures must take to accommodate
the conception of people as autonomous citizens.   This
bare account can be supplemented with comments on the role
of education as a primary good and its consequent protection as a constitutional right.   Within this framework,
of course, there will be whole areas of study and the
learning of all kinds of practical activities - from
astrophysics to basket-weaving - in which politics as such
and the kind of topics we have been considering in this
book will never occur.   (There will, however, be some explicit consideration of political matters as I indicate
below, p. 90f.) It nevertheless remains true that all
these learning activities take place within a political
framework, which in some sense provides a rationale for
them and which can be made explicit.

This is probably the point at which to dispel another
possible misconception.   I have suggested that the political rationale for the educational structure can be made
explicit but have not said anything about whether, and
how, it should be.   I pictured a child asking about the

education system only to make my point about the political
context of education more graphically.   I am not suggesting that when a four-year-old asks 'Why do I have to go to
nursery school, Mummy?' the parental response should take
the form of an abstract rigmarole about primary goods,
constitutional rights, defensible authority structures and
the like.   There are two points to be made here.   First,
it is a matter for educational judgment as to when, as
part of the child's political education, one makes explicit the political framework of the education she is experiencing.   All kinds of factors come into play here, motivational ones as well as ones to do with the level of the
child's understanding;   it would be foolish of me to
attempt to lay down pedagogical guidelines in a general,
abstract way.   This is a judgment to be made by practi-
tioners within the field of political education.
Second, we must not forget that simply by being within the
educational structure one acquires, implicitly, and by
degrees, and not necessarily in logical order, some understanding of the political structure of society, particularly as it bears on education.   This is not unique to
the participatory democracy, of course.   Many sociological commentators on our own society, like Paul Willis in
Learning to Labour, have noted what one can learn from the
organization and curriculum of the school about one's
society and one's place in it (Willis, 1977).   The difference with the participatory democracy is that for
everyone learning through the structure is a matter of
coming to understand how the system works, what one's
place in it is, what rights, obligations and opportunities
one has.   Most important of all it is a matter of developing fraternal attitudes to one's fellow citizens which
inform and give a context to all the knowledge acquired
about rights, obligations and opportunities.   In this
respect growing up in the participatory democracy is very
much like becoming a member of a club, where each member
enjoys the support and encouragement of the others in
developing her own particular interests and style of life.
This makes a contrast with political learning in the constitutional democracies we are familiar with where some
individuals can certainly acquire a great deal of political knowledge but where citizens differ vastly in what
they learn, and where there is no thread of fraternity
underpinning the whole.   In our society blacks, working-
class people and to a lesser extent, women are likely to
learn that society is indeed in some sense a club but that
to different degrees they are only associate members of it
without full status.   Certain jobs, educational opportunities and styles of life seem to be open only to full

members: those with partial status, although they have
legal and political rights, find that whole areas of the
society's life and opportunities are closed to them.   The
education system in the participatory democracy, however,
provides a context for growth into the status of a full
member of a society of fraternal, autonomous citizens.

Later, after the end of formal education the educational development of the individual continues through the
structures of work-place democracy, as she learns to
become a contributing member of a working group.   Here
again the organization of the school has given her an introduction to work-place democracy which is filled out
when she herself joins the work-force.   In many other
pects, too, participation as an adult in the institutions
of the society - leisure centres, hospitals, libraries -
will constitute a further development and refinement of
the individual's political education.   This learning will
be cumulative, with little, if anything, that needs to be
unlearned, since as we have seen the participatory democracy is all of a piece in its attitudes to its social
arrangements.   It will not be a case of learning one set
of co-operative, concerned attitudes in school only to
have to forget these when one joins an atomistic work-
force locked into an adversarial relationship with its
employers.

I have gone on at some length about the development of
the individual's attitudes and dispositions through the
structures of the participatory democracy since this will
be by far the largest and most important form which political education will take.   It is particularly important
since in this form principles, machinery and appropriate
attitudes can all come together in a coherent way.   It
cannot, however, constitute the whole of an individual's
political education both because the knowledge and experience acquired would tend to be haphazard and somewhat
patchy in its coverage of the main items with which citizens should have some acquaintance and because of the dangers of indoctrination.   It will need to be supplemented
during basic education by a theoretical or formal political education.   This will have three main elements.

(i)   It will be concerned to make explicit and available
for critical consideration the principles, attitudes and
assumptions underlying the participatory democracy, that
is values, like justice and benevolence, the fraternal
attitude and assumptions about man and society.   The
links between these bedrock principles and attitudes and

the actual political machinery of the society will also be
drawn out so that the contingent status of the latter
becomes clear.   Then arrangements for and against particular realizations of the principles can be examined.

(ii)   Relevant political knowledge, too, will need to be
made available to pupils.   All types of knowledge will
fall into this broad category - for instance, knowledge
about the political debates in which the society is currently engaged, which will include some historical account
of how these issues became politically important;   knowledge about social structure;   detailed knowledge of particular institutions;   knowledge about the international
political scene in so far as this is not already covered.

(iii)   (i) and (ii) have centred on the principles, machinery and concerns of the participatory democracy.   Citizens will, however, also have to be aware of alternative
forms of disposing of power within communities: they will
need at least some theoretical acquaintance with other
political systems.   This broader perspective will counter-
act any parochialism which might otherwise develop.   It
will also constitute some safeguard against indoctrination
in that it may do something to prevent people coming to
believe that the most desirable form of society is the
participatory democracy without ever having considered
other possible forms.

    This section on political education in a participatory
democracy is only a sketch, to give some indication of how
the constitutional right to education might, in broad outline, be implemented.   I have not attempted to go into
detail, partly because any details would necessarily be
speculative since they would be produced without knowledge
of the particular historical circumstances, and partly
because I am more interested in the forms which political
education might take now, in our society, as a means to
helping to bring about participatory democracy.   With
this rough picture of the general objectives of a political education in a participatory democracy in mind, we can
turn our attention to the detailed shape political education might assume in the here and now.

POLITICAL EDUCATION IN OUR SOCIETY

Political education in our society will have the same
broad aims as in the participatory democracy.   Of the
highest importance will be an understanding of the

principles underlying democracy and an appreciation of the
contingent status of the machinery devised to implement
them.   Relevant political knowledge will also be required.
Necessarily going along with the principles and knowledge
and of equal importance will be the fostering of a fraternal attitude amongst citizens.   Again, as in the participatory democracy, the education will have two aspects, a
theoretical one and a practical or institutional one.
The second, I want to argue, is immensely significant for
the individual's political learning.   To emphasize this I
want to discuss it first.

Political education: the school organization

In the participatory democracy, as we have seen, the content and organization of education will be democratically
controlled both nationally and locally.   We also saw that
for teachers, dinner supervisors, helpers, caretakers,
secretaries and so on schools are work-places and like
workers in any enterprise those working in a school should
be able to expect that its decision-making arrangements
for all internal matters will recognize their autonomy.
This means concretely that all those working in the school
should participate in decisions which affect their work
and be accountable to their colleagues for their dele-
gated responsibilities in the running of the institution.
I have argued for similar arrangements on general grounds
to do with the appropriate relationship between workers in
any enterprise in Chapter two.   Here I want to argue for
democratic arrangements among workers (i.e., non-pupils)
in any educational institution from the point of view of
the pupils' political education.

There is certainly room for debate over what precise
parts of political education should be the responsibility
of the school.   There is, however, one aspect of political education about which there is no choice.   Any school
must have some kind of organization, some procedures for
making decisions among its employees.   (For instance,
some things may be decided at staff meetings, some things
may be decided by the head, some decisions may be left to
individuals.)   A fair proportion of these decision-making
procedures, in turn, are bound to be known to most pupils.
There is no way in which all the procedures could be
secret or confidential.   Indeed it would not cross anyone's mind in most schools to attempt to keep them so.
It follows, therefore, that as well as learning their
French, maths, environmental studies and so on pupils are

also learning how their particular school is run.   They
are developing conceptions of authority, power, what it is
to be responsible for something, what are considered
appropriate decision-making procedures and so on.   What I
am suggesting is that if we are to provide children with
an acceptable political education we have to be sure that
we can defend our decision-making procedures and the roles
and statuses we assign to different members of the institution as the ones most suitable for a school in a democratic society.   In this connection we may need radically
to revise a common British conception of the school head.
Is it appropriate, for instance, for the head of an educational institution to be the (often) unchallengeable
determiner of both major educational policies within the
school as well as the details of the dress of its members?
Could the role of head as often presently conceived be re-
placed by administrators covering some of her functions
and, say, a school's council covering others? (see Chapter
four)

If you feel inclined to doubt what I have said about
the pupils' knowledge of the school organization, you
might like to find ways of asking pupils about the organization of their school, who decides what and so on.   In
my experience even infants' school-children give a pretty
accurate picture of the way things are, organizationally
speaking.   That being so, the important thing is that it
should be a defensible picture.   In so far as pupils are
getting a picture of an indefensible authoritarianism
they are being led into an inconsistency.   There is <u>talk</u>
of democratic ideals, practices, etc., but they <u>see</u> that
important institutions in society are actually being run
on anti-democratic lines.   A political education which
involves these unexplained contradictions and inconsistencies is clearly falling short.

It seems to me very important not to underestimate the
educative influence of a well-run democratically organized
school.   The point I am making here is essentially that
made by R.B. Haldane about the civil service in 1923 in
his presidential address to the Institute of Public Administration.   There he said:

It is not only by rendering highly skilled service to
the public in dealing with administrative problems and
questions, even of policy, that the civil servant of
the future may serve the public.   The Civil Service,
if itself highly educated, may become one of the
greatest educative influences in the general community.

It may set a high example and may teach lessons which
will have far-reaching influence.   I believe in its
own interests, not less than in those of the State, it
is well that it should set this ideal before itself as
one which is of immense practical importance in its
tendency to raise the standards in business and in life
generally of those with whom it will have to be dealing
constantly (quoted by Thomas, 1978, p. 159).

The same might be said of the day-to-day dealings of all
the staff - teachers, secretaries, dinner supervisors,
caretakers - in a school.

I now want to say something about the participation of
pupils in the school organization.   There are various
ways of viewing such participation.   One could argue for
it on instrumental grounds - if pupils are involved in
their school organization, it improves their school work -
or on grounds of children's rights.   I do not want to
take either of those lines.   Instead I want to argue for
participation as a necessary part of children's political
education in a society which aspires to be a more thorough-
going democracy.   Of course, even if you accept that experience in the running of democratic institutions is a
necessary part of political education - and I shall give
reasons in a moment for thinking that it is - you might
argue that children could get it elsewhere, in voluntary
organizations like youth clubs, sports clubs, Scouts,
Guides and so on.   I would accept that point in general.
As I have said, there is room for debate over precisely
what aspects of political education should be the responsibility of the school.   In a society rather differently
organized from our own children might well get this experience in voluntary organizations.   In our society, where
education is compulsory up to 16 - two years before people
are expected to participate responsibly in national politics - but where not every child belongs to a voluntary
organization, there is a strong case for pupils getting
their experience of participation in running an institution, in school.

Now, if one accepts that one important place for such
participation is the school, this still leaves the question: is participation in the running of democratic
organizations a necessary part of political education?

At this point it is important to recall the conception
of democracy developed in Chapter one.   Then I argued

that the presumption in all authority structures must be
in favour of direct participation in decision-making
unless good reasons can be found to the contrary.   From
that it follows that political education must prepare
people for such participation in later life.   This gives
us four reasons why the experience of participation is an
essential part of political education.

(i) The first reason is the crucial one.   It relates to
the acquisition of political attitudes, for instance,
attitudes to authorities, power, working with others and
so on.   The point about attitudes - familiar from discussion about moral attitudes - is that people do not acquire
them overnight.   Attitudes develop, they build up.   None
of us were silly unreasonable children until some magic
age at which we suddenly became reasonable, considerate,
etc.   It is the same with the kind of political attitudes
we want to encourage in democratic citizens.   People can
acquire all sorts of knowledge about democracy.   They can
learn that citizens should be, for instance, appropriately
critical of authorities, tolerant of other viewpoints,
willing to have their mistakes pointed out and to rectify
them especially if they are wielding power and so on, but
they need political experience to learn how to do these
things in context.   For instance if you say to a 12-year-
old before a meeting 'If we're going to get through all
the agenda items before 1 pm I think you will need to be
a fairly firm chairperson.   Don't stand for any long,
irrelevant contributions' she will be unable to take your
advice, even if she wants to, unless she has had some experience of attending meetings, having her attention drawn
to the way in which they are chaired and having already
had some experience of chairing meetings herself.   She
has to know how to be firm without being autocratic and
actually be able to do it - judge the right moment to
intervene in an overlong contribution and find the right
form of words with which to do it on this particular occasion.- and this, given human beings as they are, is unlikely to be possible unless she has had the opportunity
to try, and been advised and corrected on the job.   In
our society it is the school par excellence which can provide such carefully guided practice in participation in
decision-making if it shapes its school organization with
that end in mind.   The remaining three points follow from
this one.

(ii) This kind of experience of decision-making would
provide a valuable model of small-scale political organization, often lacking in the kind of political education

which in concentrating on national politics, gives people the impression that politics begins and ends with the activities of central government.   Such school experience could be useful in connection with consumer groups, residents' associations, shop-floor committees and so on, making them more accessible to people who might otherwise see them only as self-help associations for the informed and socially assured.   Providing such experience in school would allow people to develop the abilities and social confidence to permit them to function in such groups when they judged this to be appropriate.

(iii)   Guided experience of decision-making in school would also provide a yardstick against which in due course to measure the authority structure of the work-place and it would enable people to make some contribution to the organization of work-places on democratic lines.

(iv)   Properly planned school experience in decision-making, as an integral part of political education, should provide opportunities for everyone to feel that they can be politically effective, can contribute to decision-making.   This would make a not insignificant contribution to the struggle against sexism and racism in our society. In addition it would concretely illustrate ways of life in business, public administration and so on which would give people some understanding of jobs which might otherwise remain closed books to them.   Again, this would be an attempt, if only a small one, to even up job opportunities for different sections of the population.

Three objections

The above arguments will by no means convince everyone. Let me try and deal with what seem to me to be three important objections.   Before I consider these, however, there are two qualifications to be made without which there could be some misunderstanding of the position argued here.   First, I am not concerned to determine precisely what children should and should not decide and at what ages.   For reasons already explained, they will not be taking decisions about the shape and structure of the whole curriculum.   Beyond that it is not possible to go further here than the general principle that the presumption must be in favour of direct participation in decision-making unless good reasons can be given as to why that is inappropriate.   The detailed work on exactly how children can contribute to decision-making in their

schools must necessarily be done by others, taking into
account the details of local conditions. Second, what I
have outlined is certainly not to be taken as constituting
the whole of political education. The kind of experience
in decision-making argued for is only one part, although
an important part, of the whole task of political education. Now the objections.

First, it might be argued that this treatment neglects
the obvious point that politics is about power, that

> political skills, whether exercised within a democratic
> framework or not, are predominantly those that enable
> one to impose one's own views on others, and get one's
> own policy or one as like it as possible - whether or
> not one regards it as in the best interests of all con-
> cerned - translated into corporate action.... The love
> of power, the competition of rival factions - surely
> these things are absolutely typical, indeed of the
> essence of any political acitivty.

Therefore, the argument goes on, democratic participation
in schools is likely 'to prematurely whet the appetite for
power and intrigue' (Dunlop, 1979, pp. 45-6).

In one particular this is right. Any politics, as I
have repeatedly stressed, is about power in that the decisions made necessarily affect people's lives and interests,
crucially or trivially. In this sense decision-makers
may be said to exercise power over others - most obviously,
as we have seen, in compelling them to pay taxes, less
obviously, in determining what gets on to the political
agenda. This is a fundamental point which no one involved in decision-making should lose sight of. Indeed, in
the kind of experience in decision-making in schools I
have been advocating the force of this point can be
brought home to every single pupil, since, if the organization is planned intelligently, everyone will, at some
point, be involved in decision-making and therefore in
wielding power. Pupils can therefore be made aware of
the fact that they are morally responsible for the decisions to which they contribute. Far from neglecting the
point that politics is about power, my argument in favour
of experience in decision-making, actually _emphasizes_ that
point and its moral implications.

On the other hand, I would reject the view expressed
that political skills in a democracy must necessarily be
exercised with the purpose of imposing one's views on

others. Of course, in organizations which claim to be
democratic this can happen - no institution is proof
against human frailty - but there is no reason to regard
it as a <u>necessary part</u> of political life. One of the
functions of the school experience of decision-making
would be to help pupils to make judgments about the nature
of sectional interests and the common interest and their
mutual relationship. These distinctions and judgments
are among the most difficult in politics, as we have seen,
but there is no reason why pupils should not slowly build
up some understanding in this area over time so that at
least they are not limited to the simplistic view that
politics can be no more than a sophisticated means of getting your own way. Rather, they are able to consider and
aspire to a conception of politics which sees its task as
attempting to order people's lives together so as to allow
individuals to flourish in a fair and fraternal society.
Furthermore, the experience of participation can help
pupils to acquire the habits of working within the conception of politics to which they aspire. Thus the educative force of the school ethos can help them to acquire
habits and intellectual conceptions <u>pari passu</u>. My point
is, very emphatically, that there is no reason why the
school ethos should necessarily emphasize power-seeking,
thus whetting the appetite for power, rather than a concern to do what is right in the context of the whole community.

A second worry about pupils' participation in school
organization is that it may constitute a form of indoctrination or, at least, an undesirable kind of moulding. In
other words, there may be openness at the level of formal
political education - all kinds of possible forms of political organization may be discussed - but the structure of
the school will carry a determinate message: <u>this</u> is how
an institution should be organized.

Undeniably this is how things must be, I think. As I
have hinted already and as I shall argue again (see below,
p. 109f), however, one can escape the charge of moulding
pupils' views of democracy through the structure of the
school by encouraging them to appreciate this very problem. As part of pupils' political education one must
ensure that they appreciate that the school has to have
some decision-making structure. They must then come to
understand the particular one which has been devised for
their school, whatever form it takes, and finally they
must grasp that as a democratic structure it is not fixed
for all time. It can be changed in all kinds of ways.

A third and different kind of objection might be level-
led at the proposals here, not in principle but as a practical possibility.   It might be argued that although it
would be desirable to have schools run democratically, it
is not possible because teachers, never mind dinner supervisors, caretakers and so on, would not be able to cope
with the demands it would make on them.   Teachers, as
well as non-teaching staff, might find it difficult to
cope with the experience of being questioned by children,
having to justify school policies and so on.   They might
also find it hard to give pupils responsibilities for
which the pupils would be accountable.   Something of this
sort might well be true and I think it has two interesting
implications.   First, it suggests that people seeking employment in schools, in any capacity, might have to give
evidence of their willingness and ability to work within
such a democratic system.   In other words, if we are to
take these proposals seriously, superb teaching qualifications or fast typing speeds and efficient office practice
will not be sufficient for someone who seeks employment as
a teacher or a secretary in a school.   How the evidence
of willingness to work within a democratic system is to be
obtained raises questions, but if such a system is to be
introduced this will have to be tackled.   Second, there
could be training schemes for school staffs, probably of a
fairly practical work-shop nature, although - and this
goes back to the first point - for people to be considered
for schemes they would have to want to work within a democratic framework.   These are stringent demands but necessary ones if the school is fully to realize its potential
influence in creating an ethos which will foster democratic habits in its pupils.

Political education: the curriculum

(i)   In our society the education system as a whole cannot
provide the political education which it does in a
thoroughgoing participatory democracy.   The system as it
stands cannot be made explicit to pupils so as to indicate
to them their future status as autonomous fraternal citizens because it does not have that rationale.   As common-
sense observation and much work in educational theory has
made plain, our education system is warped throughout by
its selective function which overshadows all else.   From
the start of their school lives children are progressively
channelled into large occupational groupings - professional, middle class, white collar and skilled and unskilled
manual worker - and given an education which is deemed to

match their occupational status.   Solicitors, doctors and
accountants need Jane Austen, Virgil, modern history,
physics and so on, hairdressers, transport workers, hospital porters need English lessons based on their own experience, computation, art and technical drawing.   Teachers
and schools could of course make all this explicit to
their pupils as part of a political education, but it
would be wholly negative.

    As we have seen however, the essential bedrock of a
political education is a broad grounding in all the main
areas of knowledge, which will enable children to make
personal and political choices.   What can teachers do
here constructively?   Where the whole curriculum is concerned, individual teachers can do relatively little
beyond pressing for a broad curriculum in their schools
and at any other educational level where pressure can be
applied.   Individual schools with sufficient like-minded
teachers can do very much more because in the British context they have considerable curricular autonomy and so can
make conscious efforts to ensure that children enjoy a
broad curriculum.   I know a number of schools, both primary and secondary, where attempts to provide a broad curriculum for each child are meeting with considerable success.   One obvious reason for this is that people of very
different particular political persuasions can support
such a curriculum.

(ii)   Politics is not a discipline like mathematics.   It
is, rather, constituted by several areas of knowledge -
sociology, history, political philosophy, economics and
law - in its central concerns.   As well as a broad curriculum, therefore, children, if they are to receive an
adequate political education, will need relevant economic,
historical, sociological, philosophical and legal knowledge (see White, John and White, Pat, 1976).   These
studies will have to form part of everyone's course of
study, either taught independently or in an integrated
course.   They have clearly, a special status in relation
to political education.   The information and the insights
they provide are indispensable to political understanding.
Nothing can substitute for them.   If they are not available, there is just a gap in the individual's political
awareness.   Any school intending to provide a political
education must ensure that it has a well-thought-through
curriculum policy in these areas.   I suggest some elements of the philosophical component below (see below,
Political education: politics teaching: a philosophical
perspective).

(iii)   Other subjects - English, drama, music, art, science - could make specific contributions to political education.   In addition there are several reasons why it would be desirable for a school to have a 'political education across the curriculum' policy.   Let me explain how such a policy might work and the reasons for it.   First, the policy.   What I have in mind is that when the syllabuses dealing with those studies comprising politics - history, economics, sociology and so on - have been made available to the whole staff, it will be possible for teachers responsible for other areas of work to suggest, if they want to, work they might do which would relate to political education.   It is easy to think of political novels or work in science connected with pollution and conservation, but equally there may be music or art teachers who would be interested in digressing from their instrumental teaching or their object drawing to introduce political issues which bear on the arts.   I do not think it is essential for all teachers of non-political subjects to do this continually.   It would be bad if they did, since it would tend to give too great a significance to politics, as though for everyone political activity should be an end in itself of the highest importance.   However if at some once-yearly forum teachers of apparently non-political subjects are able to offer suggestions on topics or issues they would be interested to cover, these can be considered and co ordinated into an overall programme without unnecessary overlap.   The topics covered, the issues raised or the links made might occupy little time in lessons or on the time-table.   What is helpful in developing political awareness is not to be measured in lesson hours or exercise book pages but in how much it contributes to the synoptic view of the place of politics in human life.   A three-minute digression in a science or art lesson could be very illuminating coming at a certain point in an individual's developing understanding of political affairs.   There are at least three reasons, I want to suggest, for the staff to co-ordinate such contributions into an overall programme.

First, in a participatory democracy through their basic education, their understanding of the education system and its links with other social institutions citizens will have a synoptic view of politics.   This is not to say that this will be all-important to them or dominate their thought systems.   For some it may, but for most it will simply constitute one conceptual framework through which they view the world and which brings with it certain obligations.   My guess is, however, that in our society even

amongst teachers, who might be regarded as some of the
better educated citizens, there are relatively few with
such a synoptic view of politics.   Most of us I imagine
who are in any way connected with the education of young
people, whether teachers, parents, youth leaders or whatever, could benefit from a forum in which what I have suggested are the politically central subjects - economics,
history, sociology and so on - as well as the non-political ones are discussed from the point of view of their
contribution to political understanding.   This kind of
once-yearly forum is just one way in which we as teachers
might so to speak pull ourselves up by our bootstraps in
this area.   Whatever direct benefit this brings to the
political education of the pupils, there is almost certain
to be a growth in the synoptic political understanding of
the teachers.   This cannot but be an indirect plus for
the pupils.   After all, such understanding is what we are
aiming for in our pupils, and if we are to be politically
educated persons we need it too.   Acquiring it in this
piecemeal, and possibly somewhat difficult fashion, largely by our own efforts, will also offer insight into what
we are demanding of our pupils and may suggest ways in
which we might facilitate similar learning for them.

A second reason for a 'politics across the curriculum'
policy is that it is likely to make the staff a more co-
hesive and therefore more effective working group.   If
teachers have forged a common policy to which they are
committed they are likely to be more successful in achieving it than a staff who, although nominally committed to a
policy, have not talked it through.

Sceptics - and half of me is very much a sceptic - will
want to challenge this claim and to suggest that common
efforts at intellectual understanding are just as likely
to produce deep and divisive rifts amongst working groups.
That may be so and it would be interesting to study places
where this has happened because it seems to me from personal experience of working in such groups that it does not
have to happen.   What are the ingredients accompanying
communal efforts to improve intellectual understanding
which tend to produce cohesiveness?   What might be relevant is the tacit awareness that the participants constitute a group and that only through their own efforts will
a policy be produced.   It is counter-productive to mince
teaching colleagues' arguments into shreds or to use this
forum to pursue some personal vendetta.   The most effec-
~e way of proceeding is likely to be by way of construc-
~nsideration of cases.   Irrelevant points and

obviously potty suggestions are best left on one side
rather than ruthlessly exposed.   Discussions will focus
on what most people want to develop rather than on those
contributions which people regard as useless.   This, I
would claim from experience, is likely to be the kind of
situation in which communal efforts to arrive at intellectual understanding will tend to produce co-operativeness
and cohesiveness in other activities.   If I am right this
tends once again to suggest that a necessary element in
feelings of cohesiveness or what we earlier called fraternity is the intellectual grasp of a common bond with
others - here the awareness of the bond between oneself
and others as members of a group trying to achieve   certain kinds of intellectual understanding.   This of course
would explain why the fraternity continues into the subsequent activities.   It would be rather odd if it did not,
if we take it that these are directly or indirectly connected to the understanding.

     Undoubtedly we need research here, both philosophical
and empirical.   Once given these mutual efforts at understanding, to get full benefit from them we need to know
what kind of conditions produce the cohesiveness and co-
operativeness which sometimes seems to result.   Here I
have only been able to make some suggestions.

     Third, if teachers in schools do attempt to forge a
'politics across the curriculum' policy in this way, their
efforts can only serve as the best kind of model for their
pupils.   Not that they should self-consciously draw their
pupils' attention to their efforts, but, as I said earlier,
there is likely to be no way in which these proceedings
could be kept secret from the pupils.   Knowledge of these
activities will offer pupils an insight into how groups
can rationally debate and implement policies.   This may
seem a small point, but it is of the greatest importance
for political education.   Pupils, being human, are
likely to be far more impressed by one concrete example of
communal policy-making than by numbers of theoretical
lessons on participatory democracy.

Political education: politics teaching: a philosophical
perspective

The need for a broad curriculum for an adequate political
education has been made clear.   I have also argued that
certain subjects within that curriculum constitute the
disciplines which make up politics - history, economics,

sociology, law, political philosophy - and relevant parts
of these must be studied in some depth.   I want now to
focus on political philosophy in particular and on the
basis of arguments presented earlier to suggest certain
topics and distinctions in this area which would have to
figure in any education for democracy.

But before that, three disclaimers.   First, I am not
going to suggest how these topics might be taught since
speculative accounts of possible teaching methods would
not be appropriate in an essay of this degree of general-
ity, where the learners' stage of cognitive development,
the resources available and so on are unknown.   This con-
nects with my second disclaimer.   I have not yet said
what stages of education and what age of children I am
concerned with.   This has been intentional since in talking about the whole curriculum it is irrelevant.   A child
requires a broad curriculum for political education but it
probably does not matter when she studies the different
components, whether, for instance, the natural sciences
are a continuing component or only occur at some periods.
As far as the specifically political studies are concerned, I have so far only argued that they should be present
in everyone's education and have not suggested whether
they should come earlier, or later, or more continuously.
In the last section of this chapter where I make recommendations about policies for political education, I shall
argue that there are good reasons for not delaying the
introduction of political knowledge, argument and ideas
but for beginning to bring them in quite early in the
child's formal and informal education.   Third, what I am
doing here for political philosophy - namely picking out
certain distinctions and topics which would have to be
covered in any political education - is only a first shot.
The whole project would need further research and refinement, and similar work would also be needed in the other
relevant disciplines of history, economics, sociology and
law.

(i)   Of first importance for an understanding of politics
in a democratic society is a grasp of the distinction
between (a) principles and assumptions about human beings
and the world they live in and (b) the institutions which
depend on those assumptions and attempt to embody and
implement those principles.   I am not implying that this
distinction should be taught before anything else but that
it is logically rather than temporally basic in the organization of anyone's conceptual scheme in the political
area.   It is in fact a point which one could not grasp

until one had some concrete understanding of particular
institutions and their functions.   Once this learning
process begins however continual reference will need to be
made to this distinction as political education proceeds.
The reason for this should be clear.   Unless the very
different status of values like justice, fraternity, and
benevolence is distinguished from that of institutions
like the British parliament, the American congress, the
German Bundestag and so on, there is a danger that pupils
will come to see the latter <u>as</u> democracy.   Societies
which have, for instance, a parliament elected on a one-
person, one-vote basis, modes of decision-making which
involve majority voting and no imprisonment without trial
will be regarded as democracies and any societies with
different arrangements will be beyond the democratic pale.
It is also likely that if people regard a collection of
institutions and procedures as democracy, they will think
that 'making one's society more democratic' can only mean
either maintaining or strengthening those institutions.
They may see suggestions for additional or very different
structures to embody the principles as the brainchildren
of cranks or fanatics.   Things may be changing now but,
until recently, this was very much the reaction which
greeted suggestions for establishing authority-structures
in work-places on a participatory basis.

(ii)   I have argued for the need to make explicit the distinction between bedrock principles and basic assumptions
on the one hand and institutions on the other.   I need to
indicate now in broad outline what falls into each of
those categories.   Let us take the principles and basic
assumptions first.   Of prime importance for the pupil is
an understanding of political power and its place in human
life.   Here the points made in Chapter one will be relevant, the distinction between wants and real interests,
the connection between real interests and paternalism and
so on.   This understanding of power will be easier to
develop now than when I first began thinking along these
lines about political education because a number of philosophers and educational theorists have been working on
analyses of power and their application to educational
issues (see, e.g., Nyberg, 1981; Benton, 1982).   It will
need to be connected with work on two other fundamental
notions - the good for man and justice.   And open-minded
explorations of the possibilities of determining, in general, and substantially, what the good for man is will be
required.   The outcome of these will have to be connected
to the analysis of power.   Issues like the following will
need consideration: can exercises of power be justified

if they advance the good of individuals?   Can they be
justified even if they do not?   If they are necessary to
advance certain human goals, how is this compatible with
any view of an individual's good which puts a high value
on his/her autonomous choice?   These investigations will
need in turn to be linked to a consideration of the notion
of justice.   This was hardly attempted in Chapter one but
clearly the idea that each individual should be guaranteed
equal access to the exercise or control of power needs
examination.   Only my broader and more policy-oriented
interests in this essay have kept me from considering the
intricate web of notions connected with justice, notions
like equality, fairness, positive discrimination and criteria of distributive justice based on desert, merit or
needs.   A study of justice would be a prominent topic in
political education.   Linked to it, as I indicated earlier, would be a consideration of fraternity as a value.
Fraternity is a difficult notion to pin down and one
easily confused with seemingly related notions of friendship, togetherness, co-operativeness and so on.   Fraternity, however, as we saw, is the motivational undergirding
of all the basic structures of the participatory democracy
and if we are to move in that direction as a society we
need to explore this attitude and distinguish it from related attitudes which we may mistake for it.   Also needed
is a consideration of the basic characteristics and capacities of human beings as well as what capacities are presupposed to the democratic character.   This topic is
linked in turn with that of the good for man.   As we saw,
its detailed consideration will underpin arguments for
each person's need for primary goods.

It is no accident that this sub-section draws so heavily on Chapter one, for I am suggesting that each individual's political education should provide him or her with
the chance to develop a skeletal picture of the principles
and basic assumptions underpinning democracy.   In broad
outline this will take the form of the framework set out
in Chapter one - or more likely some revised version of
that framework.   I am not advocating that these principles should be taught in clinical isolation.   The purpose of this arrangement here, under headings and sub-
headings, is simply to indicate the categories to be covered in political education and to stress the distinctions
between them.   Very likely the principles will be taught
pari passu with the teaching about the institutions covered in the next section.   This is not to rule out
abstract discussion of principles but only to stress that
it is not being laid down as the norm.

(iii) If the last section echoed Chapter one this one
will do the same for Chapter two. Pupils will need to
consider the broad institutional structures which might
embody democratic principles. As we saw in Chapter two
problems to do with reconciling the equalization of access
to power with the formulation of society-wide policies
taking into account the public interest have proved a
stumbling-block for many theorists. Pupils will be encouraged to think hard about the kind of institutions
which might capture the spirit of the principles in a
defensible way. How acceptable is the system of neighbourhood groups with considerable control over local
affairs, arranged in a pyramidal structure with a body at
the top which refers its resolutions about society-wide
concerns to the national forum? There are certainly
problems with this conception and there is scope for imag-
inative alternative attempts to devise a system which
better embodies the principles.

    Power, as we saw, is exerted as much in the work-places
of our society as in government departments and town halls.
How can equal access to the exercise and control of power
be achieved here? A case was argued for the democratization of work-places. Pupils might examine it and other
schemes and discuss their acceptability as well as their
limitations. Some issues to be considered might be: are
there any general principles which apply in the case of
all work-places? Do very different arrangements apply in
the case of those enterprises supplying goods and services
on the market from institutions like hospitals, libraries,
television and newspapers, the police or the army? Or is
this a false distinction? Should all goods and services
be regarded as supplied to a market? Or should none be
so considered? The issues here are complex and merit an
airing in schools, particularly because in our society it
is hard to think of another forum where all potential
citizens could be introduced to them.

(iv) As well as considering how to make the general political institutions and work-places of our society more
democratic, pupils also need to study a number of particular institutions and issues. What looms largest is what
modes of decision-making the participatory democracy
should employ, and whether these should include majority-
voting. The main thrust of this essay has been the need
for democrats to reduce exercises of power which necessarily attack their autonomy and to make powerholders
accountable to those over whom power is exercised. The
problem is that the device of majority voting, seemingly

indispensable to decision-making in a democracy, necessarily involves exercises of power over others.   The
issues it raises need to occupy a prominent place in any
programme of political education.   Without straying too
far into the area of teaching methods and strategies, it
is worth pointing out that these issues need not be dealt
with in a totally theoretical way with pupils poring over
Pennock and Wollheim or potted versions of these, or even
worksheets on the potted versions.   The topic of majority
voting not only can be linked to practices within the
school or wider society but, if it is really to come home
to potential citizens as a problem which vitally affects
the implementation of their centrally held values, it
needs to be linked to their actual experience of decision-
making.

My own efforts in discussing the issue of majority
voting, even with adult students, suggest to me that
teachers may have to work quite hard before its problems
are appreciated - in particular the connections with power
and with fraternity.   This is not so where issues to do
with 'dirty hands' and political secrecy are concerned,
since it is easier to find telling examples from societies
pupils are familiar with.   Questions to do with the role
of and justification for civil disobedience in a democracy
also merit discussion, particularly, as we saw, in relation to some instances of the operation of majority
voting.

In this essay I have limited myself largely to what I
have termed basic education or school education.   At some
other time I would like to consider the role of other
formal educational institutions in political education -
in particular institutions of higher education.   I should
also like to examine the possible educational role of
television, radio and newspapers.   Here further questions
arise: can the media be seen as having an educational
role?   If they can, should there be any control over them
in the interests of the best performance of this role or
would this constitute undesirable censorship?   Should
they be made accountable for their programme and publishing policies and, if so, how and to whom?   Although there
has been no discussion of these issues in this essay, this
is not to say that the same policy of self-denial should
apply in the political education provided in schools.
The role of other formal educational institutions and the
media needs to come under scrutiny here too.

(v) Finally to be included in this catalogue of the ele-

ments which must figure in a political education if one is
viewing that education from a philosophical perspective,
are a number of topics of a critical or justificatory
kind.   This is not to suggest that the topics previously
discussed - from the principles/institutions distinctions
to particular values like fraternity and particular institutions like majority voting - will be treated uncritical-
ly: the stuff of philosophy is obviously argument and
counter-argument.   What I have in mind here are a number
of more general topics which question the whole rationale
of the education provided.   Perhaps the largest of these
is the justification of democracy, and particularly participatory democracy, as a political arrangement.   Linked
with this is the justification of the compulsory political
education which is provided.   Political education should
invite pupils to consider why, given the rationale for the
participatory democracy in terms of the individual as an
autonomous chooser, they are being compelled to follow a
broad curriculum which includes a political education
covering certain pre-specified topics.   The answer lies,
I suggest, in coming to understand what it is to become an
autonomous person, living among other autonomous persons,
in a society.   This will demand certain social arrangements - the participatory democracy - and in turn certain
educational arrangements: every potential citizen will
need to be involved in these.   At this point the arguments discussed in relation to compulsory political education will link with those concerning the citizen's obligation to participate in the political system in Chapter one
(see Chapter one, pp. 17-19).   Obviously related to the two
previous issues are a cluster of questions connected with
the possible indoctrinatory nature of the whole system.
As we have seen already, this is a particular problem in a
scheme of political education which is not simply a presentation of facts about systems of government and institutions but is also concerned to encourage people to develop
certain attitudes, for instance, fraternal attitudes to
their colleages and fellow-citizens and to do this, in
part, by having them participate in certain structures
which are likely to foster the development of these attitudes.   This seems to be just the environment which could
be a hothouse for the growth of attitudes and commitment
to values in an unquestioning way.   To some extent that
is right, I think - it resembles in this respect the
child's earliest experiences of home life where the world
simply is as her parents or 'gran' has structured it.
The school, whilst bending all efforts to make itself a
fraternal community, can adopt a reflexive attitude to its
efforts and encourage its pupils critically to examine the

values it is trying to promote as well as the particular
ways in which it is attempting this.   It is easy to lay
this down as a precept, of course, but much harder to
implement it sensitively and intelligently.   One has to
promote honest reflection on the values rather than indulge in a sham exercise which is in fact only a subtle
reinforcement of them.   On the other hand, the school has
to avoid purely destructive criticism which negates its
efforts to promote fraternity and caring attitudes amongst
its pupils for no good reason.   Some institutions can
seem to manage a constructively critical attitude to their
own arrangements without either becoming corrupt or des-
troying themselves in the process.   Here research into
good practice would be useful.

As a first sighting shot I have tried to indicate what,
from the perspective of political philosophy, would need
to be included in a political education in school.
Further work is called for, however, both here and in the
other politically relevant areas of sociology, economics,
law and history.

I would like to finish by considering two specific
policies in this area.

Political education in the first school

When is political education to begin?   Must it be delayed
until the upper reaches of the secondary school because
children at the primary stage are too young to grasp
principles or concepts or acquire political attitudes? (3)
I want to advance four considerations which, taken
together, seem to me to suggest that it is both possible
and desirable to begin political education in the primary
school.   The first three arise out of research done on
the political understanding and political attitudes of
young children and the last out of the nature of political
education itself.

(i)   Any politically intelligent observer can confirm that
primary school-children - from, say, six upwards - do
operate with political concepts and embryonic forms of
political argument.   Research confirms this too (see,
e.g., Connell, 1971; Greenstein, 1965; Stevens, 1982).
Children, even at this early stage, often have views about
the government, other countries and politically related
matters rather closer to their hearts, such as what counts
as a fair share, sex differences and how these might/should

affect the allocation of work roles, the amount of pocket
money an eight-year-old should get and so on.   Given,
therefore, that children are already operating, albeit
crudely, with political and economic concepts and forms of
argument, the skilful teacher has an opportunity to encourage them to reconsider and develop these.   This does
not show that the teacher should do so, but it at least
shows that in one important respect young children cannot
be said to be too young for political education as they
are already on the threshold of this way of thinking.
This combined with the second consideration gives the
beginning of a case for political education in the primary
school.

(ii)   A number of researchers have shown, mainly, but not
wholly, in the area of the attitudes of children to
foreign people, that 'quite firm likes and dislikes are
held in conditions of quite primitive ignorance' (Heater,
1977, p. 131).   In other words strong political attitudes
develop in under-11s in the absence of much political
knowledge.   It also seems that these political attitudes
remain firmly embedded in pupils' minds so that attempts
at systematic political education in early adolescence
have little noticeable effect on them.   This vigorous
growth of political attitudes in primary school-children
and their relative immunity to revision later seems to me,
along with (i) above, to constitute a strong reason for
attempting to subject such attitudes to rational scrutiny
early on.   At least we have nothing to lose by helping
young pupils rationally to assess their attitudes in the
light of appropriate knowledge.   If, as research seems to
show, later attempts are doomed, why not try at an earlier
stage to marry knowledge and attitudes more rationally?
This is surely a better policy than leaving young pupils
to form strong attitudes 'in a conceptual vacuum' (Tajfel,
1966).

(iii)   Commitment to democracy of whatever particular form
- representative or participatory - necessarily commits
one to a belief in the basic equality of all persons as
citizens.   Where political knowledge is concerned,
though, the following statement seems to sum up what is
generally the case: 'boys score significantly better than
girls and middle class children much higher than working
class.   The social class difference is greater than the
sex difference' (Johnson, 1970, p. 35).   These differences must surely disturb any democrat.   But might not a
determined attempt at political education in the primary
school do much to reduce them?   Admittedly I am only

speculating in suggesting that early political education
could have this effect, yet it seems plausible and worth
testing, given what we know about the stunting effects of
stereotypic self-images on individuals' conceptions of
what they can do.   By the time girls and working-class
children come to formal political education at the moment
- those, that is, who are lucky enough to get even that -
they are no doubt already set to see it as 'not for them'.
Society's stereotypes are too strong for the teacher's
reasoned arguments to break through.

(iv) It will not be disputed, I imagine, that all
teachers have a responsibility for the moral education of
their pupils.   Certainly the primary school teacher will
be insistently faced with this responsibility in the day-
to-day running of her classroom.   She will be constantly
reminding children - however she does this - to share, not
to snatch, to pick up rubbish they drop and so on.   More
generally she will be encouraging them to think of others
- 'To whom should we send parcels of the produce from our
Harvest Festival?   Does anyone know an old person living
alone?'   So far, so good.   But concern cannot stop with
one's family and friends and the people in one's locality.
It would be arbitrary to do so and democratic political
arrangements are attempts to institutionalize some of the
moral values which inform our relationships with our
family and friends.

But this broad application of our moral principles so
that, for instance, the moral indignation we feel over injustices is not confined only to those in our own, or even
our own national backyard, but is aroused by the oppressive treatment of people further afield, is not something
that just develops naturally as we grow older.   If it is
to develop it needs to be thoughtfully fostered.   That
this is so is shown, I think, by the indifference of most
of us in our everyday lives to the fact of the gross and
widening differences in wealth between the rich and poor
people of the world.   At government level there is obviously some awareness of the increasing divide as conferences on the issue and, more concretely, aid to poorer
nations show.   It has also been tackled in philosophical
books and articles (see, e.g., Honderich, 1980, Chapters 1
and 2; Singer, 1979, pp. 158-82).   But neither the general problem nor the amount and kind of aid which richer
nations might give to poorer ones have ever, to my knowledge, been election issues or the subject of large-scale
demonstrations in the richer countries.   It is certainly
easy to forget the problem living in a very rich country

where the facts of poverty do not impinge.   Indeed in our
national misery at our economic plight we forget that this
plight is an enviable one for most people in the world.
Would the situation be any different if a properly
thoughtful political education existed in schools which
gently but consistently widened pupils' feelings of concern for others and encouraged them to think about the use
of political machinery to tackle these problems?   For the
most part, as adults, no one has to prompt us to feelings
of concern towards our parents or children or colleagues.
We, as we say, 'naturally' help them if they are in some
kind of trouble and we are 'naturally' happy when something makes them happy.   But such concern is not 'natural' in the sense that it flows spontaneously from us, it
is something we have learned over many years from our
moral community.   What I am suggesting is that concern
could be learned for all our fellow-men.   It would not,
for all kinds of psychological reasons, be of the same
quality as that for our family and friends or issue in the
same kind of actions, which would be inappropriate.   But
if it is to be learned, an important task for the primary
school is gently but consistently to widen pupils' sympathies towards people in their own country and beyond, indicating at the same time that it is largely through political means that these sympathies can be expressed.

Some people may yet wonder whether this is not all
rather remote from primary school-children and perhaps
better left until the secondary school.   But why wait?
Primary school-children are, I have argued, intellectually
capable of this kind of concern, so it is not ruled out on
those grounds.   It might also be important to begin to
broaden children's concern for others early so that it
becomes habitual to them as much 'second nature' as concern for family and friends.   Otherwise there is a danger
if one waits until the secondary school that these concerns are seen as 'tacked on', as an optional extra which
one is not blamed for disregarding.

There is an additional point.   At a later stage of
political education one will want to discuss a number of
issues which presuppose that pupils do already feel concern for people beyond their immediate circle and even
beyond their national boundaries - issues for example to
do with priorities amongst moral responsibilities or the
rights of states to interfere in the internal affairs of
other states.   Without this concern children quite simply
will not see the moral/political problem.   Again this
argues for attempting to widen sympathies early on.

Taking these four considerations together there seems
to be a case for beginning political education in the primary school.   Children can grasp political notions at
that stage; it would be desirable to attempt to counter-
act early on the development of political attitudes without the corresponding political knowledge; starting political education earlier might do something to offset some
of the inequalities between different bodies of citizens
where political knowledge is concerned; appropriate political dispositions towards one's fellows need to precede
the intelligent discussion of political problems and might
take root better if introduced early.

Political education and teacher training

A policy consequence of the arguments presented in the
main body of this chapter and of the arguments advanced
for beginning political education in the first school is
that we need to provide specifically for political education studies in the professional training of all teachers.
This may seem an extravagant step.   Is it really necessary to prepare all teachers for this work?   Could we
not rely on specialist teachers of political education,
politics graduates and others with the politically related
specialisms mentioned earlier?   Now although, as we saw,
there is a place for specialist politics teaching, political education cannot be left solely in the hands of such
specialists.   There are at least three reasons for this:

(i)   In the first school most opportunities for the development of political understanding will present themselves
informally in the day-to-day running of the class or
school, as they do in moral education.   Skill is needed
at this stage to see a chance for political education and
use it in such a way as to build on what a child knows, to
leave her curious about political concerns and anxious to
know more, because she is getting the idea that these
things matter.   To orient the child towards the political
in this way requires the knowledge and skill that a professional training can provide: this cannot be restricted
to just a proportion of teachers.

(ii)   At the secondary stage there will be specialist
contributions to political education from teachers of
sociology, history, economics and so on, so there might
seem to be less reason to provide specific training in
political education for all secondary teachers.   But at
this stage too there is much that can be done informally.

More than this, given the importance of a broad curriculum
for political education, it is essential for teachers to
understand the role of their subject in promoting a democratic society.   As we saw earlier they should have some
understanding of how particular areas of human concern -
art, science, mathematics, etc. - inform and relate to the
political dimension.   We are demanding this of pupils as
potential citizens: we cannot demand less of their
teachers.   An appropriate training, although not necessarily an extensive one, would supply this orientation.

(iii) Finally, and most important of all, whatever the
responsibilities of any particular teacher in the political area, all teachers will need to be introduced to political education in their professional training because we
are now only too aware of what may be learnt from the
'hidden curriculum' to be insensitive to the political
implications of school and classroom organization. However much or little direct political instruction teachers
introduce, they will need to be aware of their responsibility for the political messages they may be transmitting to
their pupils by their school and classroom practice.   A
professional training in political education will help the
teacher to adopt a self-critical attitude to, for instance,
the decision-making methods she uses.   When, if at all,
does she use voting?   What might children learn from this
about the appropriateness of voting as a decision-making
device?   Again, how does she most commonly attempt to
motivate pupils?   Do attempts, e.g. to stimulate competition between pupils cut across her stress at other times
on the value of co-operation in the community?

    Let me assume that the case is established that all
teachers, both primary and secondary, should have some
responsibility for the political education of their
pupils.   Given the present state of political education
in this country is it possible to say anything in detail
about the form the teachers' professional preparation for
political education should take?   It would be arrogant to
imagine that one could lay down a masterplan all ready for
implementation.   Equally, mere hopes expressed in a
vacuum are a poor basis for further development.   Let me
therefore offer a few provisional notes.   The following
suggestions represent elements to be covered.   Not all
require equal attention, but I have not attempted to
specify the amount of time to be spent on each.   There
is also no particular significance in the order in which
the elements are mentioned and it is certainly not intended to indicate a teaching order.   What follows is not a
blue-print but an agenda for debate.

All intending teachers should be offered what one
might call the minimum essential studies for those involved in political education at any level.   This would give
them some orientation towards the political dimension of
education and it would give primary school teachers the
conceptual framework for the content they would be teaching.   The studies would include a course in political
theory which would cover basic notions like the state,
law, rights, social principles as well as the various
theories of democracy - participatory and representative.
The study of democracy would pay particular attention to
what the democratic citizen needs in terms of knowledge,
skills and attitudes to operate politically.   Certain
parts of moral theory would also be treated, for instance,
notions like 'fraternity', 'community' and 'personal
autonomy' and the relationships between them would merit
special attention.   Some relevant and basic elements of
sociological and economic theory should also find a place.
These studies, which would give the teacher a firm conceptual grasp of the political area, would be placed in a
concrete setting in two ways - by some study of recent
political and social history and by illustrative comparative studies of political education and its implications
in two or more countries.   The comparative studies would
be a valuable, integrating factor exemplifying in an
immediate and concrete way the factors studied in political theory.

This body of studies may strike some as rather abstract
and high level, especially for primary school teachers who
will be involved only in the first stages of political
education.   I regard it, however, as essential for anyone
developing children's political consciousness, especially
in the open setting of the contemporary British primary
school where so often political notions will come up informally and the teacher will need to have a well-articu-
lated framework of political and economic concepts in
order to have the flexibility to recognize and build on
the opportunities as they present themselves.   If there
are great problems of pressure on the time-table, the comparative studies could be omitted, since I see them, in
this context, largely as a way of making some of the
abstract notions more lively and immediate.   Otherwise I
see this body of studies, as forming the essential theoretical framework for teachers.

It is probably unnecessary for secondary school
teachers to do more than this but to the studies outlined
above there would be added for primary school teachers

some considerations of the content, methods and organization of political education in formal education institutions and elsewhere.   Here they would be able to familia-
rize themselves with existing curricula and also consider
what reforms, changes, etc. might be made.   As well as
considering the construction of curricula for different
ages, there would be opportunities to examine the appropriateness of different methods, e.g. explicit instruc-
tions, games, simulations, etc., for the development of
conceptual frameworks, the ability to assess political
argument and the fostering of political dispositions.
Discussion of issues connected with indoctrination, impartiality and bias would also come in here.

    I am assuming that as well as these courses followed by
all teachers there will continue to be specialized courses
for those intending to be politics specialists in the
secondary school.   These will cover the ground outlined
above (i.e., those parts not already covered in undergrad-
uate studies) in rather greater depth.   They will also
include, on the one hand, studies in the social sciences
relevant to political education, e.g. psychological
studies of attitude formation and change and sociological
studies of political socialization, etc., and on the other
some study of the particular institutions of our society
with which citizens need to be familiar. (4)

4 Headteachers: a changing role

In Chapter three it was argued that certain changes are
needed in school organization both to make schools more
democratic work-places for their staffs and to promote the
political education of their pupils.   The role of headteachers in this process of change is crucial and they
need special training for it.   In this chapter I want to
discuss the form this training might take.   This chapter
does not end like Chapters three and five with a set of
policy recommendations since the whole chapter constitutes
the detailed working out of one recommendation.

In another way too this chapter differs markedly from
three and five.   There I spend considerable time discussing, respectively, political education and the role of
parents in a participatory democracy.   It might be expected that a good part of this chapter would be an elaboration of the role of the headteacher in such a society,
but this is not so.   The reason is simple.   There would
not be headteachers, as we know them, and therefore
special heads' training programmes would not be required.
In a participatory democracy there would be training for
the whole staff in school organization and the role of the
'head' would be radically different from that role in our
society.   Framework guidelines for the curriculum of the
school and its organization would be determined by the
central decision-making body, the national forum, and as
far as school organization is concerned, as we have seen
already, the guidelines would specify that the whole staff
would be responsible for the running of the school.
Beyond that the guidelines would probably only indicate
forms of organization which would be ruled out (e.g.
arrangements which totally excluded pupils, or in which
all decision-making was left to one person), leaving the
detailed arrangements to be decided by the staff them-

selves.   This might result in 'head-like' roles being
created, but with important differences from the ones with
which we are familiar.   In some situations, for instance,
there may be administrative chairpersons with a limited
term of office, in others several limited-term chairpersons with responsibilities for different aspects of the
work.   Any arrangements, however, which fell within the
broad guidelines covering school organization and which
were subject to review and modification by members of the
institutions would be acceptable.   For this kind of system
to be workable, however, all staff would have to be prepared for it.   This would involve some introduction to it
in their initial professional training and some subsequent
in-service training.   There is nothing more of a general
sort for me to say about such training and, given the fundamental importance of personal autonomy in this account,
it is for the participants to settle the details.

Heads in our society could, however, benefit from
special training programmes.   Many people will think that
in these days of very large schools with perhaps 2,000
pupils and 150 staff, heads need at least some kind of
'management training' to cope with the administrative,
financial and personnel problems they are likely to face.
But I want to claim that they need something more.   All
too often the assumption of 'management training' courses
for heads - the kind of short courses run by LEAs - is
that the head needs to be helped to develop skills and
techniques to run a good, harmonious school with few staff
or pupils' problems.   To this end courses concentrate on
interviewing techniques, time-tabling, ways of delegating
routine work to leave oneself free to cope with major
trouble-shooting, and even perhaps the latest group dynam-
ics theories so that one can get one's 'body-talk' right.
This however tends to take for granted, and therefore
leaves unexamined, the context of the head's work and what
it is he or she could, or should, be aiming at.

It is all well and good, however, to talk about the in-
adequacy of 'management training' programmes and to say
that they should be supplemented; but can one get away
from tedious clichés about 'the need for heads to engage
in fundamental reflection on the aims of their work' and
specify concretely what form such reflection might take
and how it might figure in a training programme?

To see how courses might be structured, extended or
supplemented, one needs to look at the reasons which might
be advanced for encouraging heads to reflect upon their

role.   The reasons are all-important because the kind of
case that is made will determine the content and even the
pedagogy to be used in the training.   With this in mind
let us look at three cases.

THREE CASES FOR TRAINING HEADS

(i)   The consistent head

There is first what might be called the minimal case for
heads' training.   It might be agreed that this should go
beyond the nuts and bolts of time-tabling, etc., to re-
flections on the nature of the job because this is implied
in the role itself.   However one conceives the role in
detail, the head must be, _inter alia_, an administrator
and, as such, she must work according to principles which
enable her to operate consistently.   This is not easy
because she has to be both consistent over time and in
respect of her dealings with different groups, governors,
advisers, colleagues, pupils, parents and so on.   This is
the kind of thing sometimes probed at appointing committees when a prospective candidate for a headship is asked
what her personal 'philosophy of education' is.   When
she reveals her views, she is pressed with further questions like 'If you incline towards a child-centred view of
education, would it follow that you would do X?'   Sometimes, of course, the point of these questions is to find
out exactly what the candidate means by a catch-all phrase
like 'child-centred education', but it is just as likely
that the point is to see how far she has thought through
her views and how far they form a coherent set of principles.

There is some pressure, then, for the head to get her
principles into order and to see to what she is, or is
not, committed.   This is, however, in two ways a very
minimal claim.   First, and more trivially, it is minimal
in the training demands it makes.   In many cases one
might need to do no more than urge heads to get their
views into some consistent shape.   More important, it is
minimal in that it will not necessarily involve any reflection on the whole framework of one's beliefs.   It may
be that the drive for consistency will cause some people
to reflect on their fundamental assumptions about educational institutions, authority relationships, conceptions
of children's abilities, etc., but it need not do.   A
head might well formulate her own educational principles,
perhaps on the basis of certain religious convictions,

without ever questioning this basis.   In that case her
views may be thought through, able to be implemented without any internal contradictions, but rest on unquestioned
assumptions.

   The head needs, then, to be consistent in her beliefs
and practices, but to pitch the demand for training at the
level of the consistent head is to pitch it far too low.

(ii)   The linch-pin head

The second case I want to consider is the dynamic head who
keeps abreast of contemporary educational developments.
What one might call the 'linch-pin' conception of the head.
Anyone espousing this case will find the minimal view of
the consistent head outlined under (i) literally archaic.
An advocate of this second view will suggest that in the
British autonomous, decentralized educational system,
where the head has so much de facto responsibility for the
running of the school, she must be able to reflect on the
often conflicting aims of education canvassed in our
society, if she is to direct the running of the school on
properly educational lines and, for instance, encourage her
staff to pursue profitable lines of curriculum development.   The merely consistent head is totally inappropriate to run a school anywhere in Britain today.   The problems of our society are such that the woman who has simply
got her own views into some sort of order will be unable
to deal adequately with the kind of conflicts of values
which will be forced upon her attention as a head.

   These conflicts will occur in various contexts.   With
staff, whose views conflict with her own, the head will
need to be able to debate the viability of different conceptions of education.   There may be agreement amongst
colleagues that the school should educate its pupils for a
multi-cultural society but sharp disagreements on inter-
pretations of what it would be to do this.   The head must
be in a position at least to understand this debate and at
best to attempt some resolution of it which results in a
defensible multi-cultural policy for the school.   With
governors too the head may well find herself having to explain and justify school policies and, as a consequence,
having to participate in a wider discussion of the aims
and objectives of education.   In so far as parents come
with complaints to the head, these may well contain,
implicitly at least, different conceptions of the aims of
education from those of the school or, more likely,

different priorities amongst aims.   Once again the head
needs to have reflectively considered what is involved in
aims like education for independence, self-realization,
the world of work, or happiness.   To be in a position to
understand, help and advise parents, she needs to have
examined the assumptions underlying aims like these, their
possible justifications and how, if at all, they are to be
related to one another.

As well as coping with conflicts, however, the head
will also have to adapt school policies and practice in
the light of governmental policies and other external
pressures.   At the present time, for instance, she would
need to think how she might protect her conception of the
school curriculum from the impact of falling rolls and
government cuts.   Even in happier times, however, there
would be the constant flow of government and schools
council documents into her in-tray to await her judgment
on their applicability to her particular context.

Advocates of this second view often have their own
cases of actual heads who are wonderful examples of what
training with these objectives should produce at its best.
They are described to one as 'a very bright young man,
who's transformed the school in three years', 'a wonder-
fully dynamic head', or 'an intelligent woman, knows what
she wants from her staff and absolutely dedicated to the
school'.   A visit to a school run by one of these super-
heads usually bears out all the claims.   There exempli-
fied in this individual, who is usually brimming with
energetic resourcefulness, is intelligence, dedication,
determination and considerable knowledge about the impact
of central government and local authority policies in her
area.   Questioning usually reveals that this knowledge
and these qualities are indeed used to inspire staff,
resolve internal conflicts and negotiate tactfully with
parents, so as to exploit every opportunity - and even
some reverses - for the educational good of the school.
What more could one want of the head of an educational
institution of whatever size?   If training programmes
could be devised which would produce heads of this
calibre, would not any society, with even moderate resources to spend on education, have to regard their support as a good investment?   Paradoxically, perhaps, I do
not think so.

At this point we need to look at the reasons why anyone
would support the kind of training programme which aims at
producing the knowledgeable, resourceful head.   I labelled

that conception of the head the 'linch-pin' view, for that
is indeed what she is: the prime mover, the initiator,
the Athene of the institution.   Someone holding this view
would see the head's position as the key one in the institution and in recruiting to the training programme would
look for people with 'leadership qualities', which the
training could enhance and channel appropriately.   The
final realization of this ideal would be, I suppose, a
whole educational system with an appropriately trained
head steering each institution.   These heads would form
the élite corps of the educational world, leading and
inspiring their colleagues and pupils.   This conception
of authority relationships within the educational system
is however quite at odds, I would claim, with what is
appropriate to a democratic society.   It is contrary to
what is required by democratic principles of the authority
relationships in any institution and, in the educational
context, it will have a mis-educative effect on pupils.
Some people may find the comments on the undemocratic
character of the 'linch-pin' conception of the head uncon-
vincing.   It may seem to them that one can hold a view of
the democratic society which is not at all at variance
with this conception.   I can best attempt to deal with
such doubts by delineating the third conception of the
head.   This is developed by contrast with the second and
involves a brief reminder of what I am taking to be
implied by democratic principles.

(iii)   The democratic head

The third conception I am labelling the 'democratic' conception of the head's role because it is appropriate to an
educational institution in a society which aspires to be
democratic.   By a society which aspires to be democratic
I mean one which is attempting to organize itself according to the democratic principles set out in Chapter one
but one in which those principles are not as yet anything
like fully realized in all areas of the society's life.
Clearly societies can be more or less far along the way to
democracy and progress may be uneven as between different
institutions and aspects of the society's life.   Let us
assume therefore a society patchy in its commitment to
democratic principles and their realization.

It is clearly unnecessary to repeat here a detailed
characterization of a society run on democratic principles
but since, as I have said, the reasons supporting conceptions of the head's role are all-important, the view of

democracy must be briefly outlined as a reminder because
it constitutes the case for the third conception of the
head's role.   That views rests basically on twin assumptions.   (a) The first is that there are no authorities
on the good life for individuals.   No one is in a position to tell another individual authoritatively that she
should pursue for instance the active or the contemplative
life or that she should become a well-balanced all-
rounder.   That judgment must be left to the individual
who is aware of the options available and the significance
of her choice.   This assumption gives rise to a connected, subsidiary assumption, namely that there are a number
of things which any individual must consider to be goods,
since they are necessary to making and attempting to
realize her choice amongst possible options.   These are
goods like wealth, education, freedom of thought and other
civil liberties, the rule of law and the right to participate in the exercise and control of power.   (b) The
second assumption is related to the exercise or control of
power mentioned under (a)   The assumption made by this
view of democracy is that no individual has any 'natural'
right to stand in a power relationship over others.
Therefore there should be an equal right to share in the
exercise of power.   In those cases where equality in the
exercise of power would defeat, or at least seriously
damage, the realization of justice or freedom in other
ways, it will be necessary to move to equality in the <u>con-
trol</u> of power, the second-best situation, where the representative wielders of power are accountable to their constituents.   The other goods mentioned under (a) could be
administered impartially for the population by a benevolent despot; but what makes this a <u>democratic</u> conception
is the demand for equality in the exercise, or control, of
power.

   This brief résumé will suffice as we consider the role
of the head in a society which aspires to be democratic
but is only patchily so.   This, I believe, is the case
with our society.   It is patchily so in the educational
area in that we do not have the kind of democratic guidelines, argued for in Chapter three for the content and
organization of what goes on in school.   Nor do we have
any clear rationale for what should be left to central
direction and what to teachers, parents, the local community and so on.   The question I want to put is: what is
an appropriate role for a head who accepts the kind of
democratic principles set out in Chapters one and two but
works within our present society?   Crucially, how will
she differ, if at all, from the linch-pin head?

In many respects the democratic head will share the
latter's characteristics.   Ideally, she will be dedicated, resourceful, determined, knowledgeable about government policy as it is likely to affect the educational
system and her school in particular and so on.   The difference comes in the ends towards which she directs her
dedication, determination, knowledge and the rest and, it
follows, the attitudes which she takes towards her own
role, her staff, governors, parents and pupils in pursuing
those ends.   Given her commitment to the democratic principles outlined above, she will want to work towards an
educational institution in which there is equal access to
the exercise, or control, of power amongst members and in
which the pupils are at least introduced to this conception of the democratic society.   Let me give four instances to indicate how this commitment might get application
in our society.

(a) First and foremost, the democratic head will attempt
to involve all staff and pupils in the running of the
school.   This will require considerable trial and error
to find the best kind of machinery in present circumstances to share power and to make those responsible for certain aspects of the school's work accountable to the other
members of the school.   It certainly will not mean a
jumbo-sized school council meeting daily and discussing
everything from the abolition of French from the curriculum to whether girls should be allowed to wear trousers to
school.   This is clearly foolish and the kind of decision-making body which would be inappropriate in any
institution.   Unfortunately it is the kind of apparatus
which is sometimes found in schools and which brings
efforts at democratization into disrepute.   It is not for
me to attempt to draw up a blue-print for appropriate
machinery for the exercise, or control of power in very
different situations.   This must be the responsibility in
the first instance of the staff and older pupils of the
school.   Staff including head and older pupils rather
than head alone, because no democratic head will think
that there is any reason why she should impose her conception of the appropriate machinery.   And staff and older
pupils rather than staff and all pupils, because the
former are likely to have more knowledge about the work-
ability and effectiveness of different sorts of machinery.
This is, however, only in the first instance.   Once in
operation it will be open to any member of the institution
to criticize the machinery and suggest improvement.
Appropriate review procedure and arrangements for amendments, modifications and so on will obviously be built
into the apparatus.

Some people may feel that what has been lost here is
the possibility of what they may term 'genuine leadership'.
Interpreted in one way this is right.   If one is thinking
of the dynamic leadership of the linch-pin head then this
is indeed incompatible with the democratic conception,
because there is no place for a head who runs her school
in what I might call the entrepreneurial manner.   Incompatible attitudes must be at work here.   The head cannot
on the one hand be working towards a devolution of power
and responsibility so that some members do not arbitrarily
impose arrangements on others and on the other take the
kind of action and adopt the attitudes of the best kind of
benevolent head of a family firm.   It is worth noting
when talking to heads how often they talk about 'my staff'
and also how often the staff in such a school will refer
with affectionate reverence to the head, much as their
grandparents might have done to a good employer.   And
these are the attitudes in 'good' schools with 'good'
heads.   Authoritarianism need not have an ugly face and
yet it is authoritarianism for all that.

In another sense, however, the possibility of leadership
has not been lost, but enhanced.   In an institution run
on democratic principles there should be increased opportunities for individuals to exercise 'genuine leadership'.
In saying that I am assuming that by such leaders people
have in mind dynamic individuals who are able either to
describe ends, or strategies for achieving ends, in such
a way that other people are inspired to think that there
might be something in them or that they might be possible
to achieve.   The organization of the school on democratic
lines will present ample opportunities for such 'inspira-
tional' leadership without tying it to a person or an
office, so that the leader's suggestions can be subject to
debate and can stand or fall on the persuasiveness of the
case made for them.

In the arrangements for decision-making and the devolution of power within the school it might be thought that
parents have been forgotten.   This is not the case.
Since they are not in any sense members of the institution
they do not have the right to participate in its internal
decision-making arrangements.   However, as part of their
responsibilities towards their child's education, they
have certain rights to comment on these decision-making
arrangements from an educational point of view.   These
are mentioned under (d) and in Chapter five.

In connection with the proposed moves towards equality

in the exercise, or control, of power, there may be doubts
about the head's legal position if she devolves power over
matters for which she is ultimately responsible, like, for
instance, the appointment of staff or the expulsion of
pupils.   There are two points to be made here.   First,
in many aspects of the school's work and organization it
will be possible and straightforward for the head to
arrange decision-making procedures which give equal access
to power and which do not affect her legal responsibilities at all.   It is all too easy for people in positions
of responsibility to accrete more powers and responsibilities to themselves without this being in any sense necessary.   A useful exercise therefore for any head attempting to run her school on democratic lines is to see in
detail just how much of the power she now exercises can be
shared without this affecting her legal responsibilities.
Second, there are those matters where the head is legally
responsible and could in the final resort lose her job if
it was judged that she had acted irresponsibly.   Here it
is useful to make a distinction between those cases where
the Authority's Articles of Government for schools lay
down that certain matters are the head's decision, or the
head's and governors' decision, alone and those cases for
which the head is held ultimately responsible.   As far as
power-sharing goes, there is clearly nothing to be done
about those matters falling into the first category.
Anyone taking on a headship and also holding the view that
these things should be not solely for the head's and governors' decision will have to accept that this is one way
in which the society in which she lives is only patchily
democratic.   The second category presents a more difficult problem, for matters falling under it could in principle be decided by staff, or staff and pupils, as long as
the head was prepared to accept responsibility for the
decisions taken.   The general line that should be taken
here can, I think, only be left to the individual decision
of the democratic head.   It is clearly a difficult situation in that in a more completely democratic society the
assignment of responsibility would be very different and
therefore whether the head decides to devolve decision-
making, or not, she is struggling to arrange the running
of the school along democratic lines in highly unfavour-
able circumstances.   It must be left as a difficult moral
choice for the individual to decide in the light of the
particular circumstances in which she finds herself.
Having, however, made her decision on the general line she
will take, she will make this and her reasons for it plain
to staff, pupils, parents and so on.

There is a further point on the legal position of the
head.   The head, or head and staff, may be left with
decisions to make, for instance, about the broad structure
of the curriculum, which in a more completely democratic
society would be matters for decision by the whole democratic community.   Again, in the imperfectly democratic
situation they can only make what seems to them the best
decision, whilst at appropriate times and places making
the case that this decision should not be left to them
(see Chapter three, pp. 81-7).

An advantage of progressing towards more democratic
educational institutions via heads training programmes is
that much of the nuts and bolts restructuring of the decision-making machinery will be a slow trial and error
affair which ought to be started as soon as possible.
Heads are in an excellent position to take the initiative
here: training programmes can encourage them to do so.

(b)   The democratic head will want to do more than clarify
her own ideas about the aims of education in a democratic
society.   She will want to offer opportunities for the
staff, pupils and the wider local community to discuss
these matters.   But not at all in the same spirit as the
linch-pin head.   The linch-pin head debates with staff,
discusses with parents and so on because, as the major
determiner of school policy, she needs to know what others
are thinking and to persuade them of the desirability of
the courses of action she is proposing.   This is why,
within her own terms, the linch-pin head is so effective.
Careful preparation of the ground beforehand ensures that
there are no, or very few, confrontations.   Likely opposition is investigated and coped with in advance.   The
democratic head needs, however, to try to promote discussion of the aims of education and the best arrangements
for realizing these as a necessary adjunct to the power-
sharing she is committed to.   People cannot, after all,
be expected to make decisions unless they have both the
necessary factual information and also, a chance to consider what their aims are, how those aims relate to one
another, what the priorities are amongst them, and so on.

In promoting reflection on, and discussion of, the aims
of education, the democratic head is, as I said, acting in
a different spirit from the linch-pin head.   This is
clear from an observation of the activities she promotes.
Heads with this perspective are anxious that teachers,
parents, pupils, etc. should think seriously about the
aims of education but they do not feel that they have to

'manage' this in any sense.   It does not have to go on under
their auspices, as it were.   Such heads are happy to encourage their staff to go on courses at teachers' centres,
polytechnics, institutes;   they are happy for their PTAs
to organize discussions;   and for their staff to discuss
with parents the aims, teaching methods and organization
of the school.   In line with their whole conception of
education in a democratic society they feel no need to
stagemanage these kind of discussions and tend only to
take an active role reluctantly when this is the only way
to spark things off.

(c)   The democratic head will also be keen that pupils
should take a more active role within the school, both in
the management of their own and others' learning and in
the organization and running of the school itself.   I
have suggested under (a) and in Chapter three that this
will be so, but it can well be underlined again because
for pupils such participation will be a part of their
earliest formal political education.   I am not suggesting
that all pupils should be involved in every decision made
in the school because in some cases their extreme lack of
knowledge might militate against some of the basic aims of
education in a democratic society.   However, when the
spheres in which pupils may participate in decision-making
have been determined, the head will not immediately aban-
don efforts to involve them in the running of the school
if the first ventures in this direction lead to their
taking what seem to the head and staff foolish or short-
sighted decisions or lead to them becoming aggressive or
troublesome.   Learning to exercise judgment in the conduct of practical affairs is not something that is done in
a week or two.   Neither is acquiring the appropriate attitudes to one's colleagues.   Just as no one would expect
to walk into a school and find stacks of exercise books
filled with flawless work, so no one should expect to hear
of schools which run like clockwork with pupils exercising
the judgment of a Nehru or a Kissinger and demonstrating
the attitudes of a Martin Luther King.   That children
make mistakes, are prejudiced and intolerant in their
judgments, etc., can never be reasons for giving up
attempts to involve them in the exercise of power in educational institutions because those are the places par
excellence where misperceptions and inappropriate attitudes
can be corrected and redirected through the structure
itself in innumerable subtle ways with least damage to
self-esteem.

(d)   This point follows directly from the last one.   We

have been considering how a school run by a democratic
head might differ from a school run by a linch-pin head.
In respect of the political education pupils receive
through the organization of the school itself it will be
totally different.   I have argued in Chapter three that
as important as any formal instruction in political education is what pupils learn through the way the school
itself is organized.   In this I am including not only
those parts of the organization in which the pupils participate but, just as important, those in which they are not
involved.   For within a short time any pupil (even an
infant school pupil) will be aware of the organizational
structure of the institution, who is the most powerful
person, or persons, in it, who can safely be ignored as of
little account and so on.   So the pupils of a linch-pin
head and those of a democratic head (if we could imagine,
for a moment, 'pure' examples of those two categories)
would be literally living in different political worlds
and learning quite different things about hierarchy, the
distribution of power in institutions, ways of making
decisions and so on.

It is at this point that parents come into the picture.
Whilst they have no rights to participate in the organization of the school, they do have a duty as monitors/co-
ordinators of their child's educational experiences to
make sure that, inter alia, the institution is not affecting their child adversely (see Chapter five, pp.
This is obviously an aspect of school which teachers will
monitor independently but the parent is in an almost un-
rivalled position from which to get a very clear picture
of his child's perception of the organization of the
school.   It may well be a misperception of the way things
are, but that is irrelevant.   In the kind of democratic
society we are envisaging, the head and staff will be keen
to hear any comments on the organization of the school
coming from parents directly, or from parents via children, because this is one of the ways in which they can
evaluate the educational impact of the school's organization on children.

I have tried to indicate the aims and attitudes of the
democratic head, stemming from her understanding of democratic principles, and I have attempted to indicate, as
concretely as possible, how such a head might work within
our kind of society.   I want now to suggest the kind of
training programme which might be appropriate to encourage
the development of such heads.

TRAINING PROGRAMMES FOR HEADS

Let us look at training programmes for heads with regard
to their content and form, looking at content first.

(i) The democratic head needs to be aware of democratic
principles. (1)   This means work covering all relevant
aspects of democratic theory - different traditions of
democracy (elitist and participatory), majoritarianism,
criteria for citizenship, freedom of expression and the
necessary social arrangements to ensure it, dissent within
a democracy, and the role of education.   These topics in
turn will lead into work on the kind of ethical notions
which might support democratic conceptions.   This will
mean work on autonomy, utilitarianism and different conceptions of a person's interests and the public interest.
What is emerging here, in other words, is the need for a
political and social philosophy course.   One element of
this will, however, need to be treated as a large topic in
its own right.   That is education.   Possible aims and
conceptions of education - education, for instance, for
the good of the individual or for the good of society,
both of which can be conceived in various ways - will need
to be examined and priorities amongst them considered.
Different possible realizations of those aims in different
historical societies will need discussion.   This work,
particularly that in political and social theory, can
fruitfully draw on work in the neo-Marxist tradition, like
that of Habermas and Macpherson, as well as that which is
firmly within the liberal democratic tradition, for as
Tucker (1980) and others have shown, there are certain
convergences of interest between those traditions which
are missed by anyone who confines herself to one of them.
This general theoretical work needs in turn to be applied
to actual situations in actual schools.   An ideal situation for this is the discussion by heads from the same
locality, in a work-shop setting, of the implementation of
democratic principles and aims of education in their
schools.   The common background of experience and the
considerable overlap of problems encountered is likely to
contribute significantly to the usefulness of such sessions, especially if by some device, like role-playing,
they can be turned into 'brainstorming' sessions, where
ideas can be tried out without those involved necessarily
being seen to be committed to them.

(ii) This last point edges us from the content of the
course towards its form.   This is just as important,
because the participants can learn as much which is

relevant to their jobs from the form of the course as from
its content.   The course should be run on a participatory
basis, with participants determining the topics, their
order of priority and, to a large extent, by whom they are
to be tackled, i.e. whether there is to be an input by an
'expert' lecturer or by participants contributing seminar
papers.   This 'participatory' approach is vital if heads
are to get the feel of participation and to know what it
is like to run an enterprise, relevantly similar to their
own, on such lines.   This is not a trivial point or an
optional extra.   It is the heart of the training programme, for such participatory experiences are relatively
rare in our society.   Interestingly in the pioneering
work in heads' training in Sweden which was begun in 1976
this element was neglected and in the first report on that
training (Ekholm, 1977) Ekholm comments that the school
leaders taking part tended, because they were not consul-
ted about the programme, to slip into the familiar role of
passive student.   This is unfortunate both from the point
of view of their own learning and because of what they
failed to learn about what it is to be part of a self-
managed enterprise.

I have indicated what must constitute the bare bones of
content in a heads' training programme and what form such
training must take.   I have also implied that an organized course is required.   This leaves unanswered a number
of questions which I will attempt to answer now.

One might ask: why an organized course?   How long
should a course be?   And should it be compulsory for all
heads?   The query 'Why an organized course?' almost
answers itself in the light of the point made above about
its participatory nature.   If one arranged a programme of
reading, and essay writing, perhaps even with tutorials,
covering the topics outlined above, the vital experience
of participation would be lost.   In one sense the participatory course is part of the content and the same programme cannot be offered either as an organized course or
by correspondence or whatever.   The second question of
how long the course should be breaks up into other questions of whether such a course should be a standard aca-
demic course covering a term or a year, full-time or part-
time, or whether it should have some other format.   What
is best here will clearly be in part a matter of trial and
error, finding out what formula produces the best results.
The Swedish programme I mentioned takes twenty-five days
spread over two years in short bursts of two to four days.
In between the participants are in their schools, usually

with certain problems to resolve relating to their own
institutions.   Given the nature of the course this is
probably a useful format.   The very modest heads' course
we have been trying in an experimental way in the depart-
ment where I work has been run on a part-time basis, with
heads from the same local area coming, at their own
choice, after school and occasionally for whole day-
schools. (2)   This format seems to allow for the reflective arguing through of issues whilst keeping theory
closely tied to practice.

Should such courses for heads be compulsory?   In
Sweden the courses, which overlap somewhat in content with
that outlined in (i) above, are compulsory and by 1985 all
Swedish heads will have participated in such a course.
In any society which is aspiring to extend the application
of its democratic principles courses on aims and conceptions of education in a democratic society probably will
be compulsory because such a society will be anxious to
enlist the help of its headteachers in discussing how it
might best further its development along democratic lines
and also on the role of the school in this process.   A
society less dynamically democratic may permit such courses but not make them obligatory.

Questions of a different sort might be raised about who
is to teach these courses and what disciplines they will
draw on.   Although some of the issues raised in them will
stray into other areas, they have their natural home
within philosophy of education and in the overlapping and
closely related studies of political philosophy and
ethics.   When I referred above to 'inputs' of lectures
from experts I was thinking of people working within philosophy of education with a particular interest in the
ethical and political foundations of that study.   Whether
these courses are run as discrete units or as part of a
larger training programme including other sociological and
administrative courses relating to the heads' work, is
another matter to be decided by reference to particular
circumstances and the provision already available.   These
issues, however, to do with the aims of education and the
nature of a democratic society fall within the field of
philosophy of education and need to be approached by
people who have been philosophically trained and are used
to looking at educational issues and problems in the light
of that training.

Is the suggestion, then, that people trained in philosophy and working on problems within the philosophy of

education are the real democrats who are going to train
the young generation, via their headteachers, into democratic ways?   No.   The role of the philosopher of education is that of an expert who can be immensely useful to
people pondering on the desirability of different political arrangements.   She can demonstrate to them the need
to understand what is involved in an exercise of power,
and the cases that can be made for different distributions
of power within a society, including the democratic case.
And she can help them to acquire the philosophical skills
to assess such cases.   The philosopher is not the 'real
democrat' training up others in her likeness; but she can
provide indispensable tools for democrats.

CONCLUSION

My conclusion is mainly concerned with strategy.   Let me
put the question in this way.   If the main objective is
to move as quickly as possible to the establishment of
more democratic educational institutions in which there is
equal access to the exercise, or control of power, is the
best means to this training programmes for people who are
currently heads?   Such people, it might be argued, may
have been motivated to apply for their headships for
reasons which make the idea of sharing power with their
colleagues peculiarly unpalatable to them.   In addition,
the habits they will have learned in office are likely to
make them resistant to the values and associated attitudes
of participatory democracy.   Why, it might be asked,
advocate this uphill path towards more democratic educational institutions?   One could, after all, argue that
there should be legislation establishing guidelines for
school organization like those suggested above, and in the
process simply cut out the role of head as we know it.
In this way one avoids having to persuade people in
attractively powerful positions to adapt and restructure
those positions so as to give up as much of their power as
possible.

Anyone who is convinced that our educational system
could be more democratic can campaign for legislation to
enable it to become so by joining pressure groups, using
the press and television to put the case and so on.
This, however, does not rule out taking other action in
the meantime.   Campaigns for legislation and heads'
training programmes can go on side by side.   There is
every reason indeed for them to do so.   Acquiring democratic attitudes is not like acquiring even a moderately

complex skill - in mathematics say - which one might
expect to master in a few hours with a competent teacher's
help.   For many reasons, some to do with the great range
of application of such attitudes, learning to be democratic takes time and requires the help and encouragement
of other democrats.   Constructing appropriate democratic
machinery can also be a slow business as attempts are made
to fit institutions and practices to principles.   If,
therefore, the restructuring of our educational system via
legislation is to be a success, there must be opportunities for us, who are to work within it, to learn to build
up democratic attitudes and practices.   In saying this, I
am not denying Edgley's claim (1980) that education is not
sufficient to bring about a more thoroughgoing democracy
and that structural changes within society are needed.   I
am simply making the point that for those structural
changes to stick, those living and working within them
have to want them, and want to further and develop them.
Providing heads' training programmes now is one way of
introducing heads and their colleagues to the possibility
of extending democracy and getting some of the problems
involved in its extension considered.

At this mention of heads and colleagues someone, whilst
agreeing that campaigning for legislation does not rule
out action in the meantime, might argue that that action
should not be simply heads' training but whole staff
training.   To which I would respond: why not indeed, if
local authorities can be persuaded to allow such programmes and release the whole staff of a school for such
a purpose?   That indeed is another route to the further
development of a more democratic educational system.

I am simply advocating the heads' training route as a
possible one, which may recommend itself for eminently
practical reasons, to anyone who favours making a start
now.   This suggestion is a practical one in two ways.
First I am suggesting that it may be easier for local
authorities to release heads for the limited periods indicated earlier rather than whole staffs of schools.
Second, I am assuming that a heads' training programme
has, course for course, a potentially wider effect on the
educational system than a whole staff programme.   Heads
involved in such programmes can be expected to go back to
their schools and start to initiate amongst their colleagues considerations of how their particular institution
might be run along more democratic lines.   In effect the
heads themselves are playing a crucial link-role in a
wider school-based training programme.

The claim is then that heads' training programmes are a
means towards a more democratic educational system (even
if not necessarily the best means - if there is a best
means) and one which we can try now.   Provided that there
are no obvious reasons for thinking that this route
towards a more democratic society actually obstructs the
realization of that objective, should we not at least try
it?   Ultimately, of course, the test of such programmes
is whether the participants' schools do indeed become more
democratic.   It is not in the end any claims which I, or
anyone else, may make but what actually goes on in schools
run by participating heads which is the decisive evidence
for or against such training programmes.   Therefore perhaps the best way to test this claim is to establish some
experimental, either nationally or locally sponsored,
heads' training programmes and subsequently subject the
schools from which the participating heads come to an
evaluation.

Parents' educational rights and duties 5

This chapter attempts to establish a policy on parents'
educational rights and duties which citizens of a democratic state at a certain level of economic well-being
would want to adopt.   This policy, it is suggested, will
have two linked aspects.   First, citizens will lay down
certain guidelines on parents' rights and duties.
Second, complementing these rights and duties, and in consequence of them, certain duties towards the education of
young members will be established which will devolve on
the whole community.

   This is not a biological treatise and so I am not
understanding 'parents' here simply as the producers of
the .child.   'Parent', as I understand the term, is the
name of a certain social role, which differs between
societies.   In this social sense, the role of parent, and
its appropriate rights and duties, cannot be determined in
isolation;   it is necessarily linked to the political form
of the society in which it occurs.   This point can be
illustrated from the classical political theorists.   In
Plato's Republic, for political reasons which do not need
to be rehearsed here, Guardians are not parents to their
individual children but to the whole class of Guardian
children.   Hobbes and Locke with their differing conceptions of a minimal state assume the existence of independent parents and families competing for resources, with
the state as arbiter.   So does Nozick, Locke's latterday
admirer.   In Hegel's political theory the family plays an
important role as a kind of social building block, fostering certain attitudes in the citizen.   In much contemporary work in philosophy of education, however, the existence of shadowy parents in the background is simply
assumed and the kind of political theory in which they
find their place is left unexamined.   The several

attempts which have been made in philosophy of education
to establish the rights and duties of parents have started
from the biological fact of conception and have tried to
hang whatever rights and responsibilities the author would
like parents to have on that.   I hope this chapter will
show that that way is doomed because no defensible
rationale for parental rights and duties can be determined
independently of the political context.   But such
rationales are the exception.   More common is an unre-
flective assumption of parents with certain rights and so
on, particularly in discussions of equality of educational
opportunity.   Mary Warnock's reference to parents is
worth quoting as an example;

> To remove the concept of the ladder may well be to
> remove hope, and, it must be said, hope extends natu-
> rally to one's children's lives, perhaps even more than
> to one's own.   Many people feel it is wrong or in-
> appropriate to aim for too much for themselves, but
> these same people would feel purposeless and futile if
> they could not aim to 'better' their children.   For
> the satisfaction of this desire, the ideal of equality
> of opportunity remains essential (Warnock, 1977, p.
> 46).

Against the assumption that parents have rights to
'better' their children, it is worth setting Hegel's
doubts about parents' rights.

> civil society has the right and duty of superintending
> and influencing education, inasmuch as education bears
> upon the child's capacity to become a member of
> society.   Society's right here is paramount over the
> arbitrary and contingent preferences of parents, ...
> (Hegel, 1942, paragraph 239)

and in the addition to that paragraph:

> Parents usually suppose that in the matter of education
> they have complete freedom and may arrange everything
> as they like.   The chief opposition to any form of
> public education usually comes from parents and it is
> they who talk and make an outcry about teachers and
> schools because they have a faddish dislike of them
> (Hegel, 1942, p. 277, addition 147).

How is one to assess these opposing views?   What rights
do parents have?

Before I try to answer this I ought to set about determining what is meant by 'a right'.   Some will find it
shocking that I am going to take the short way with this
notion. (1)   In this chapter when I say that someone, or
some official body, has a right to do X or receive Y, I
mean simply that there is a rule permitting them to do X
or receive Y.   The justificatory backing for the rule
will in turn determine the kind of right involved.   In
other words such rules with legal backing are legal
rights, those with moral backing (assuming such to be possible) are moral rights.   This is a fairly rough-hewn
notion of rights, then, which incorporates the distinction
between the rights of the citizen and welfare rights but
little else.   It is sufficient, though, to allow us to
make some headway with the substantive issues.   It is
thus justified on the principle that one should not load
oneself down with vast amounts of philosophical baggage,
if one can manage with a conceptual toothbrush.

Let me begin with rights often taken for granted in our
society, those which allow parents to withdraw their children from the RE provided in state schools, which permit
them to send them to a fee-paying school of their choice,
to enrol them for dancing classes, piano lessons and so
on.   What is permitted is very different but these rights
can all be queried on the same grounds.   There is, first,
the possible infringement of the children's autonomy and
the possible damage to their interests by their parents'
directing their lives in these ways.   Second, even if the
exercise of these rights is in the <u>child's</u> interests,
other citizens also have interests, which may be infrin-
ged.   It is questionable, for instance, whether the existence of public schools (like ours, with the access to
positions of power which they provide for their alumni) in
a society aspiring to be a democracy is in everyone's
interest.

Should one conclude then that parents in a properly
democratic society have <u>no</u> rights over the education of
their child, because such rights may infringe either those
of their offspring or those of other citizens?

This seems to be a wild conclusion.   It seems to deny
parental rights which would be regarded as matters of
common sense;   for instance, my right to discuss my
child's progress or lack of it with her teacher, the right
to know what report the head is sending to my child's secondary school about her, the right to know why my daughter
must play with beanbags when the boys in her class are

taught to play football - and many more such rights.
They are, however, I will claim all derivative from
duties, relating to the child's education.   Basically
they all derive from a duty given to parents in our
society to take some responsibility for their child's education.   This provokes three questions in the context of
a properly democratic society;

1 What are the interests which children have which give
   their parents certain duties?
2 Must the resulting duties necessarily devolve on
   parents?   What is the rationale for this?
3 Have parents in a properly democratic society any
   rights where their children's education is concerned,
   unconnected with these duties?

These questions provide the programme for the next section
of this chapter.

PARENTS' DUTIES AND RIGHTS

What interests do children have which give their parents
certain educational duties?

Perhaps the best way into this question is to consider
what might be in a child's interest in a democratic
society at a certain level of economic well-being.   I
have argued in Chapter three that in a democratic society
what is in the public interest and the individual's
interest is a moral/political education which will enable
her to act as a responsible citizen of her society.
This includes a basic general education covering the various areas of knowledge and experience, e.g., mathematics,
the human and physical sciences, history, the arts, as
well as a specific introduction to political concepts and
forms of argument and the opportunity to acquire relevant
political knowledge and experience.

   The child, however, is not only a potentially responsible citizen but also a morally autonomous person.   This
is a basic assumption in this account of the democratic
society.   As we have seen, it is the mainspring for the
political arrangements.   It follows therefore that educational arrangements must provide the conditions for the
development and flourishing of autonomous persons.   Without such provision there would be no point in the political arrangements since their explicit rationale is to provide a context in which morally autonomous people can live

together.   There is of course an overlap here: the basic
education will provide opportunities for personal, as well
as citizenly, development.   However, in a democratic
society at a certain level of economic well-being - a
vague phrase I chose deliberately to cover societies some
distance above subsistence level - there will be further
activities, perspectives and ways of life beyond basic
education, to which citizens will want children introduced.   This will be so because a basic general education, whatever that is finally determined to cover, and
however well it is done, can only give the barest indication of the range of human activities and perspectives on
the human condition.   A child can only benefit from the
opening up of broader possibilities if she is, as a
morally autonomous person in a democratic society, encouraged to form her own conception of the good life.

Democratic citizens will want then a basic, broadly
based education set in a moral and political framework,
plus opportunities to appreciate, reflect upon and, in
some instances, participate in some of the variety of
human activities and ways of life.   I have said nothing
yet about any institutional provision of this education
but I will say something about it now.

It is useful to make a distinction here between (i)
those things which can only be taught if one has a
detailed, intimate knowledge of the educand, her state of
mind, motives and feelings and a close personal relationship with her and (ii) those things which can be taught
without having this knowledge and standing in this relationship.   This is a rough distinction because every
teacher needs to know something of her pupil's state of
mind.   But a teacher of, say, German can find out in her
first meetings with pupils how much they know of the language and, using a mixture of common sense and elementary
psychology, can work out how to interest them in learning
the next stages of the language.   She does not need to
have a close personal relationship with her pupils.   The
success of the various BBC language programmes underlines
this.   But the BBC could not teach a baby her first language or the beginnings of her moral education: this has
to be done by someone standing in a personal relationship
to her who knows her mind, attitudes and feelings in
detail, because such teaching has to take advantage of the
moment. (2)

These two types of teaching (i) and (ii) do not exhaust
the possible forms education can take because people can

learn without specific teachers from the ethos of society
and its institutions and in other ways too.   This has
important consequences.   Because education for any individual comes from a variety of sources there is a need for
someone to monitor and co-ordinate these experiences in
the early stages of education to make it a coherent whole
for the pupil and, very important, to help her to assume
the responsibility for this co-ordination and monitoring
for herself.   This demands a person with an intimate knowledge of the educand.

In any society it will be possible to have professional
teachers to teach what falls under (ii) above.   But who
is to be given the job of (i) and the job of co-ordinator/
monitor of the child's educational experiences?   It is
tempting to say 'parents'.   But on what grounds?

What duties, if any, must devolve on parents in consequence of the above proposals?

The answer in a properly democratic society would run
something like this.   As a matter of fact most people
seem to like having children and bringing them up.   They
enjoy family life and a great source of their sense of
leading a worthwhile life comes from bringing up their
children, teaching them all kinds of things, playing with
them and so on.   This seems to be true of most human
beings.   Therefore in determining who should perform the
duties under (i) and assume the role of monitor/co-ordina-
tor, one can rely on this natural fact and give parents
the relevant duties.   The rationale for giving parents
these duties becomes clearer if they are specified in a
little more detail.

They cover (a) the parents' responsibility for that
part of the child's education which depends on intimate
personal knowledge of her and a personal relationship
with her.   I am assuming that this includes at least
early learning of the mother tongue and early moral education but these are not exhaustive.   They cover (b) the
duties of co-ordinator/monitor, which are of two types.
There are (b, i) duties of an intermediary kind between
formal educational agencies and the individual child.
These can relate to the child's ability to cope with the
school curriculum.   It would be a parental duty to find
out, say, why a child is apparently falling behind her
peers in mathematics.   They can also have to do with the
school's organization.   Given that this has an important

part to play, as we saw in Chapter three, in the child's
moral and political education, parents might need to consult with teachers about, say, their child's reluctance to
take part in a school council, or her cynical attitude
towards it or perhaps her desire for a more authoritarian
set-up.   Then (b, ii), the duties of co-ordinator/monitor
also require the parents to introduce the child to the
myriad activities and perspectives on the good life which
go beyond basic education.   This point is developed
further below (see p. 164f).

It hardly needs to be pointed out that most parents
most of the time will not experience these duties as irksome, since they will be things they naturally want to do
with or for their children.   Sometimes, however, it will
be very much a matter of duty, e.g., to turn out in bad
weather, missing half of a favourite TV programme, to
escort one's daughter to the electronics workshop at the
local community centre or to have to discuss with an iras-
cible teacher what seems to be professional neglect in
respect of one's son's work.   It should not be assumed,
though, that parents will be shouldering these duties,
pleasant or otherwise, totally unaided.   A democratic
society will want to provide guidelines on parental duties
and information where necessary about how to fulfil them.
It will also want to monitor their performance and provide
help to enable any parents falling short to come up to the
mark.   I say something about guidelines, parental education and monitoring in the final section of this paper
when discussing duties of the state complementary to
parental rights and duties.

I have assumed that parents have these duties deriving
from the need to ensure that children get what is in their
interest because they seem naturally to want to bring up
their children.   (Foster parents would have the same
duties since they have, by formal contract, assumed the
parental role.)   I assume too, that they want, for the
most part, to do this in nuclear families.   If, however,
at some point, this is no longer true and either parents
want to live in extended family groups or isolated single-
parent families become the preferred mode of family life,
then the assignment of duties outlined will have to be re-
considered.   There is in other words nothing logically
necessary about parents' undertaking these duties.   As
things are there is a convenient fit between the existence
of certain duties and people who naturally, for the most
part, want to perform them and are in a position to do so.
If that position changed citizens in a properly democratic

society might well think that duties hitherto assigned to
parents would have to be re-examined.   I say more about
this in the final section when discussing the state's duty
to monitor family arrangements.

We can now see where in the properly democratic society
parental rights come in, namely as derived from duties to
do with that part of education requiring intimate knowledge and a close personal relationship with the educand
and in connection with the duties involved in the co-ordi-
nator/monitor role.   This chapter is concerned only with
general principles and I cannot specify exhaustively what
these rights might be.   They might, however, include
moral and legal rights permitting parents to require educational agencies to give them information about their
child's educational progress.   They might involve moral
and legal rights to certain resources, financial or otherwise, to enable them adequately to pursue their job of
mother tongue teaching or moral education.   Again,
parents would have to have moral and legal rights to correct their children and, in certain circumstances, to
punish them, although the forms that punishment can take
would no doubt be circumscribed.   These rights would all,
so to speak, be 'enabling rights', enabling parents to
perform duties in the child's interest.   They would thus
all be derived from those duties.

Have parents in a properly democratic society any rights
where their children's education is concerned, unconnected
with these duties?

There seems to be something counter-intuitive, against
common sense, about the position discussed so far where
parents have rights only in connection with the duties involved in those parts of the child's education which require the educator to stand in a personal relationship to
her and those involved in the role of co-ordinator/monitor
of the child's educational experiences.   Do parents not
have the kinds of rights I mentioned earlier - to select
single-sex or co-education, to bring up their child as a
believing member of a religious faith, to send their child
to a private school?   They must, one might argue, have
these rights - trumps, as Dworkin puts it, to protect the
child's interests when faced with unacceptable and mono-
lithic state provision.   For instance, the legislative
body of a community may decide on rigidly sexist schools,
Outward Bound type institutions for boys, finishing
schools for girls.   Surely it could then be argued that

parents should have the right to send their child to a
non-sexist private school staffed by liberal teachers.
Similarly, should not devoutly religious parents have the
right to withdraw their child from the secular state
school in favour of a school were religion is interwoven
with all other aspects of life?   Again there might be a
situation where a private school is realizing the aims of
education outlined above much more adequately than the
available state school.   In that situation should not
parents have the right to send their child to the school
they judge to be the better?   Again, have not parents who
detect an unusual musical talent in their child the right
to select an education for her centred on the development
of this talent?   Then there are the parents who want to
introduce their child to their own enthusiasm, say, for
collecting hat pins, going to concerts, or playing
cricket.   Do not parents have this right?   It would seem
to be a curious society in which parents had no right to
introduce their children to their interests and enthusiasms.

Let us look specifically at these examples and the
broader issues they raise.

(i)   As is perhaps becoming apparent, in the democratic
society envisaged, the problem of state educational institutions being deliberately sexist in their educational
programmes or organization will not arise.   A sexist education offends most deeply against the principle of personal moral autonomy.   It is particularly offensive because
it is likely to be pervasive and entrenched for any individual, making it very hard for him, or her, to detach
himself, or herself, from its effects.   This is brought
out very well by Sharon Bishop Hill describing the case of
the liberal couple, Harriet and John, when considering
their daughter's education.   John is clear that women
should not be deprived of economic or political rights,
nor humiliated or degraded.   However,

What he envisages is a world in which these injustices
are eradicated but one in which women remain sensitive,
understanding and charming, and in which most take up a
domestic life while most men take up a paying vocation.
Since he thinks it only efficient to prepare people for
these likely different but quite natural futures, he
thinks sound educational policy calls for certain
subtle differences in the training of males and females
(Hill, 1979, p. 121).

Sharon Bishop Hill goes on to show that Harriet's sense
that her daughter would be wronged by such an education is
a well-grounded one.   Such moulding and shaping of her
daughter would offend in explicit and subtle ways against
the principle of self-determination.   (Self-determination
is used in much the way I have been using moral autonomy.)

    In a democratic society, the rationale of which is pro-
vided in large part by the idea of moral autonomy, education will not be intentionally sexist.   In so far as
sexist elements inadvertently creep in - and with the best
liberal will in the world that is all too easy - anyone
could, and should, draw attention to them.   Parents have
a particular duty here which falls under their second set
of duties as co-ordinators and monitors of their child's
educational experiences.   It is, however, a duty rather
than a right, it should be noted, and one which would
apply of course in a less than perfect democracy like our
own.   The reverse applies too.   Parents have no right to
give their child a sexist education.   John, in the
article, has no right to bring up his daughter to be
'ladylike in figure and personality' and in just the same
way would have no right to bring up a son to be tough and
masculine and perhaps protective towards his mother and
sisters because they are females.

(ii) Similar arguments can be used against devoutly religious parents, if their intention is to bring their child
up in such a way that the child sees herself unquestion-
ingly as a religious person.   This again is to foreclose
options which it is difficult - though not as difficult as
in the sexist case - to open again later.   In the kind of
democratic society I have described, parents would have no
right to send their child to a school which was permeated
with the values, attitudes and doctrines of a particular
religion - Moslem, Christian or whatever - and where children were expected and encouraged to become believing members of the faith.   In fact in such a society there would
be no such schools for the young, although as many religious establishments for adult members of the population
as the proponents of particular religions chose to set up.
The society is not an anti-religious one, nor an intolerant one, it is simply concerned to safeguard the moral
autonomy of its members.   That concern demands special
care over educational provision so that the child's development is not predetermined in some arbitrary way by an
influence which manages to capture him at an early stage.
I have singled out an education permeated by religion in
this way because this is an option in our society at the

moment and one which parents, if they are concerned with
their child's moral autonomy, have no right to choose.
Needless to say, the same strictures would apply if specialist 'scientific schools' existed, where the whole practice of education was permeated by a scientific, technical
attitude and the aim was to turn out people who regarded
scientific knowledge as the only true knowledge and the
'scientific attitude' as the attitude which should properly inform a person's dealings with his fellows as individuals and citizens.

It hardly needs to be stated that the democratic citizen, who is against schools committed to turning out
believers, is not of course against religious - or science
- education as a necessary part of every individual's education for autonomy and democratic citizenship.

It may be of course that parents represent their position as that of people not having a right, but a duty to
bring up their child in a certain faith, perhaps a duty
falling under their general duties as co-ordinators/moni-
tors of their child's educational experiences.   If so,
then the argument goes back again to the question of
whether anyone ought to induce some very particular conception of the good life in someone else.   In other words
the onus is on the parents to show that this particular
conception must take priority over the ideal of moral
autonomy as an educational aim.   This would presuppose
the existence of moral experts (see Chapter one, p. 10).

(iii) The question of the parents' right to introduce
their child to their own enthusiasms and interests follows
on from this.   Let us assume that there is no question of
forcing on the child some very particular conception of
the good life.   The parents, interested in Baroque music,
collecting cheese labels or World War II military decora-
tions, are asking simply that they should have the right
to introduce their children to the joys of their hobbies.
This seems not only unexceptionable but positively desirable.   How else, after all, do we develop enthusiasms
than by being taken to football matches, opera houses or
junk shops by enthusiasts?   There are, however, two qualifications.   First, in conceding this I have not conceded
a special parental right.   Parents merely have the right
of anyone in the democratic society to talk about their
interests, invite others to ask them more about them, take
others along, where appropriate, to exhibitions, shows,
etc.   It is just that parents are likely to be able to
exercise this right in relation to their own children

rather more since the children are in a position to be
aware of their father's and mother's interests and hobbies.   It is in fact a right, stemming from a more general right to freedom of expression.   There is no peculiar
parental right to mould one's boy into a Liverpool suppor-
ter, for instance, as the practice of some parents might
suggest.

Second, this right that a person has to talk, etc. to
others about her interests, with of course, the usual
prima facie caveats about the appropriateness of the occasion, the listener's willingness to be drawn into the subject, etc., has to be slightly modified in the case of
young immature people.   The right has to take into
account the child's stage of moral development.   Interests which may be permissible for adults, aware of the
dangers they bring with them, may not be so for children.

At this point someone might accept these qualifications
in the abstract but suggest that they, particularly the
first, do not take sufficient account of the facts of
family life in our society.   Children, after all, grow up
in families where parents tend to take them for the kinds
of holidays, outings, etc. which they, the parents, enjoy
and appreciate especially as the children grow older.   In
many cases they hope that the children too, will become
enthusiastic campers, concert-goers or whatever.   I do
not think, however, that this constitutes any difficulty
for the position I have argued.   It is in the nature of
family life that it must for some time be shaped by the
desires and preferences of the parents but they should be
aware of their position and their rights here.   As the
younger members mature and themselves have settled preferences, there is no reason why the desires and preferences of the parents should prevail in a situation where
some collective solution (rather than everyone going their
own way) is required.   Indeed in their handling of the
family situation, where different preferences for activities and outings obtain, reasonable parents take the
opportunity to show that there are no parental rights to
shape family life so that it imposes on all members a particular conception of the good life.

A final more general qualification.   It is perhaps
important to stress that in this sub-section I have been
concerned with the issue of rights in this area of interests and hobbies.   In our society parents - particularly
middle-class ones - often take their children in the
school holidays to various exhibitions, plays, films,

musical entertainments and so on.   In so far as these
trips are conceived to have an educational aspect - and
they may well be just fun - then I think that this would
rightly be conceived by parents as part of their <u>duties</u>.
They would see themselves as broadening their child's
interests or whatever - although few parents represent it
to themselves in this rather formal, dessicated way - and
in my classification this would then fall under their
second bundle of duties as co-ordinators/monitors of their
child's educational experiences.

(iv)   Another situation in which it might be claimed that
parents have rights to determine their child's education,
can be seen as a mirror-image of the last case.   Here it
is not the <u>parents</u>' interest or enthusiasm but the child's
which is relevant.   Parents detect in their child some
gift or - to represent the facts as they more usually
seem to be - are overwhelmed by the realization of their
child's consummate talent in some particular field like
music, dance, athletics.   The child shows a great passion
for the activity, considerable skill and artistry at an
early age, with the potential to become, very likely, a
first-class performer.   To achieve such a level of performance, however, special training is required from the
age of four or five or so - ballet school, special music
lessons supported by six hours' practice daily, or many
hours spent in the swimming pool along with the requisite
regimen for building up stamina.   Attendance at a conventional school with all the demands on time that the
attempt to provide a broad, well-balanced education makes
would not permit the full flowering of this talent.   Have
not parents the right to place their child in an environment where her talents can be allowed to develop to the
full?   It does not seem to me that parents have such a
right.   What would be the basis for it?   Clearly not the
assumption that parents know best what would constitute
the particular conception of the good life which their
child should come to adopt.   This would go quite against
the grain of a society which places a high value on moral
autonomy.   One might argue that parents have a right to
facilitate the bringing about of the child's <u>own</u> choice of
a particular way of life, but this can hardly hold for the
four-year-old dancer or six-year-old violinist.   Yet it
is at the early stage that parents usually want to claim
the right to put their child in a talent-developing situation.

   To suggest that parents, qua parents, have no rights in
this context is not to solve the real problem here.

Confronted by a highly musical (or gymnastically inclined
or whatever) child, who is to decide if that child should
be allowed, or even encouraged, to devote herself for a
considerable part of each day to the development of that
talent?   It may well be to the benefit of the whole community that a supply of highly trained and gifted dancers,
musicians and gymnasts is assured, but what of the individuals who enter these rigorous training programmes at an
early age?   It seems hard to avoid the suggestion that in
some cases particular conceptions of the good life are
imposed on them.

Some may object that although the problem is a real one
the difficulties I am raising are not.   For two reasons.
First, most children who have this kind of exceptional
musical or gymnastic talent are only too happy to be
allowed to exercise it and, as a matter of fact, most find
that their adult lives, as concert pianists or whatever,
do realize a possible conception of the good life for
them.   After all, for most of us there are many possible
variations on the good life.   We would be fulfilled
living a considerable number of different lives;   it is
not an all-or-nothing affair.   These exceptional individuals are satisfied with their lives as they have developed, although this is not to say that nothing else would
have been possible for them.   Second, responsible parents
and teachers try to ensure that other options are not
closed to them.   This is done by ensuring as far as possible that the specialist training goes along with a more
general education so that the child who later comes to
feel that she has made the wrong choice has a basis from
which to work towards alternative choices.   Along with
this, responsible parents of budding gymnasts or concert
pianists try to bring home to them as they mature the
implications of the kind of life they have chosen so that
they are able to appraise their likely future with a deep-
ening understanding of all it involves.   They are then in
a position either to reject that way of life or self-
determinedly to embrace it.

There are three comments to be made on these objections.   The first objection need not detain us, since it
is an empirical one.   If it is the case that for most
children guided into the life of dancers or athletes that way
of life does become a self-chosen one, then the difficulty
I raised about imposition is largely dissolved.   Whether
it is so or not, must wait what will have to be rather
delicate investigations.

The second objection indicates a very clear parental
duty falling under the parents' general duties as moni-
tors/co-ordinators of their child's educational experiences.   This, as we have seen, is a duty for all parents
and for parents of exceptional children it gets a special
application.   They have to make sure not only that
options are not closed to the child because she is having
a specialised training, but also that she is aware of the
kind of life-pattern to which she is committing herself
and what it is, and is not, compatible with.   This will
have to be done with appropriate sensitivity to the
child's level of intellectual and emotional development.
This illustrates again that these monitoring/co-ordinating
duties should be the concern of people who know the child
well - usually the parents.

Finally, what has still not emerged is who, or what
body, has the right to place the young child in the talent-
talent-developing environment.   But in the democratic
society we are assuming this may be the wrong sort of
question to ask.   We have to remember that in such a
society people are not interested in who has the right to
direct others' lives since they do not believe that such
rights should exist.   The question is rather: who has
the right to offer the child certain opportunities which
bring with them the possibility that they may have harmful
effects on her overall development and which therefore, if
taken up, necessarily give her educators certain important
duties?   Put in this way, it seems likely that in such a
society citizens will take the view that any of a child's
educators, qua educators, should have the right to ask
whether she should have a specialised training.   Since
this is an important issue, it should then be discussed
between all those involved in her education, parents,
teachers, gymnastic coaches, etc., and a solution arrived
at which attempts to safeguard the child's autonomy in the
face of the dangers we have noted.   It would follow, too,
that citizens of such a society would have to devise machinery to be used in the case of a complete failure to
agree on what course should be taken.   We need not pursue
here the form it might take.   It is likely, however, that
it would err on the side of keeping options open, so that
where there was strong doubt about whether a child should
follow a specialised training she would probably continue
with a broad education.

It might be suggested that since specialised training
carries dangers with it, the democratic society might
forgo the heights of excellence in ballet, musicianship,

gymnastics, etc., and not permit its children to receive
such a training whilst very young.   This is an under-
standable objection given the weight I have suggested this
society puts on personal autonomy and also the dangers to
that ideal represented by early specialization.   But members of the society will also take into account that for
some people a life of dedication to a particular art or
sport will embody their conception of the good life.   In
some cases this will necessitate an early training.   It
seems to me that they will be prepared to countenance
this, given certain safeguards.   I may be wrong about
this, as about other recommendations made in this section.
But however the society tries to solve the problem in
general it is clear that it cannot be solved by assigning
to parents the right to direct their child's future.

(v)   We come now to the parents' right to remove their
child from the state school and select a private education
for her.   In this connection Brenda Cohen notes what has
been agreed 'at an international level ... to be of fundamental moral importance' (Cohen, 1978, p. 122).   She
quotes Article 26(s) in the United Nations' declaration of
Human Rights, which states: 'Parents have a prior right
to choose the kind of education that shall be given to
their children' (Cohen, 1978, p. 122).   She quotes, too,
from the European Convention on Human Rights, Article 2 of
the Protocol, which runs:

> No person shall be denied the right to education.   In
> the exercise of any functions which it assumes in rela-
> tion to education and to teaching, the state shall res-
> pect the right of parents to ensure such education and
> teaching in conformity with their own religious and
> philosophical convictions (Cohen, 1978, p. 122).

She notes the stress in both statements on the parents as
the ultimate authority in educational matters and goes on
to claim that

> although these parental rights might to some extent be
> met within a state-provided system, the possibility of
> opting out of that system is an essential safeguard
> against the degeneration of apparent guarantees of
> parental rights into a mere sham - paper rather than
> real entitlement (Cohen, 1978, p. 123).

Brenda Cohen is aware that evidence of present and historical consensus on parental rights does not constitute an
argument for them.   She suggests, however, that evidence

of such consensus at least undermines the position of
those who hold that there is a self-evident moral objection to private provision of education.   This, I suppose,
is true if stress is put on the self-evidence of the
objection.   It clearly cannot be self-evident if there is
evidence of so many dissenters.   For this defence of private schools to get off the ground, however, it has to be
shown that such parental rights exist.   This Brenda Cohen
does not do.   Can one show that there are - perhaps must
be - parental rights to select private education in a
society which aspires to be a democracy?   This question
needs to be examined in two different contexts: in the
fully-fledged democratic society based on moral autonomy
and justice, and in the imperfectly democratic society.

     In a fully-fledged democracy is there a place for pri-
vate schools?   As we have seen, a basic belief of its
members is that no one has the right to determine what
shall constitute the good life for another person.   It
follows that parents do not have the right to try to
determine the particular form their child's future shall
take.   This rules out the rationale for several types of
private schools.   Schools, for instance, which aim to
bring up their pupils to be stereotypic men or women are
excluded (as we saw in (i) above), as are schools which
aim to make pupils into adherents of a religious faith
(see (ii) above).   Whilst there may be certain kinds of
specialist education, perhaps given in specialist institutions, for the musically, athletically gifted and so on,
these are not privately-funded institutions and it is not
(as we saw in (iv)), the parent's right to select her
child for such an education.   What scope does this leave
for private schools?   Could it leave room for institutions like the public schools in our society?   Could not
a democratic society support the possibility of alternative schools to the state ones for those parents who chose
to send their children to them?   Not, it must be clear,
if those schools really are 'like the public schools in
our society'.   The morally autonomous citizens we are envisaging could not accept a system whereby parents could
pay for children to acquire certain life-chances, with the
result that powerful positions in the society tended
always to be occupied by a limited social group: in our
society Church of England bishops, Cabinet Ministers,
governors and directors of the Bank of England and so on
come predominantly from public schools.   Citizens would
have to reject such a system in favour of one in which the
chance to acquire the knowledge and develop the qualities
of character (e.g., the ability to exercise power

responsibly) necessary for such positions was not arbitrarily limited to those whose parents chose, and were
able, to pay for them.   To do otherwise would be contrary
to the basic principles of moral autonomy and justice.
It cannot therefore accept the basic principle lying
behind private schools, namely that parents have a right
to determine their child's education because they can pay
for it.   The ability to pay cannot provide a ground for
the moral right to determine the kind of education a
person shall get.   Even if, in a case where state education has deteriorated, the private education is very much
in line with what is considered appropriate for the development of autonomous people, democratic citizens cannot
allow parents' ability and willingness to pay to determine
which children are to be allowed to develop in this way.
This would be to allow an irrationality into their
arrangements - to say there are good reasons why children
should have this education but whether or not they actually get it depends on whether their parents will pay or
not.   As Bernard Williams points out, 'reasons are insufficiently operative; it is a situation insufficiently
controlled by reasons' (Williams, 1962, p. 122).   The
democrats we are envisaging could not accept it.   Like
Williams, they would want to make the reasons why someone
should have a certain education both relevant and socially
operative.   To do otherwise would be to undermine the
just and rational basis of their society.   For these
reasons citizens will seek other means than private
schools to keep their education system up to the mark.
This is not the place, and it is not my business, to speculate about what form such machinery might take but there
are clearly options like inspection systems, commissions
of inquiry and so on to be considered.   It is important
to remember too that parents, as co-ordinators/monitors of
their child's educational experiences, will have a duty to
try and ensure that educational provision is of the appropriate kind and quality.   In so far as an educational
institution is falling short in some respect there will be
informal and, if necessary, formal ways in which parents
will be able to try and do something about it.   I have
mentioned this above and in the concluding section I also
say something about how parents may be advised and supported in their efforts by state agencies.   This is, so to
speak, the 'institutional' side of their activities but
there is also, of course, the question of what they can do
in the here and now for their own child in the situation
where the child is getting an inadequate education in a
formal educational institution.   As we have seen, there
is no question of parents having a duty to send their

child to a private school, but this is not to say that
there is nothing they can do whilst the unfortunate school
situation is being sorted out and remedied.   This is not
quite the formidable task it would be in our society since
schools are by no means the only educational institutions.
There are, as we shall see, many other possible arenas for
educational activities - libraries, hobbies workshops, art
and craft centres, television programmes and so on.   In
the fully democratic society, then, there is no place for
private schools and parents have no right to send their
child to one.   They do, however, have a duty to attempt
to improve institutional provision for their child where
they find it to be falling short and a duty to make for
their child the best educational arrangements they can in
the circumstances.

Let us turn now to an imperfectly democratic society.
Let us suppose that private schools exist there, as they
do in our society.   Parents have a legal right to send
their children to them.   Have they a moral one?   Clearly
for this question to be an interesting one we have to
assume that the parents are morally responsible citizens
who aspire to live in a fully fledged democracy.   Let us
assume further that, convinced by arguments similar to
those used here, they accept that qua parents they have no
right to determine their child's particular conception of
the good life.   They wonder, nevertheless, given their
conception of their parental duties qua co-ordinators/
monitors, whether they do not have a duty to send their
child to a private school.   They represent to themselves
the dilemma in which they are placed in this way.   The
state schools to which they can send their child fail, in
various ways, to live up to the aims of education to which
a full-bodied democracy might aspire.   The schools might
be sexist, bent on making religious converts, bent on
moulding their pupils in other ways, or might simply offer
poor learning situations with much disruption.   These
defects are clearly different and I will need to say something about these differences; but for the moment let us
ignore these.   Parents might feel that they ought to send
their child to a private school which embodies the aims of
education as they see them.   But they are not clear that
their duty unequivocally lies this way because they also
accept Bernard Williams's arguments about the basic irrationality of not making the relevant reasons for giving
people education socially operative.   There is no good
reason why their children should receive this education -
which there are good reasons for all children to receive -
simply because they have the money to pay for it.   As a

reason for giving children education, parental wealth is
irrelevant.   If they support the private schools they are
supporting an educational structure which militates
against the kind of democracy they hope to see develop.
On the other hand, they reason their situation is not that
of parents in a fully-fledged democracy faced with an
inadequate state school.   Those parents have all kinds of
ways in which they can register their grievances about the
shortcomings of the institution.   They also have all
kinds of strategies by which they can further their child
child's educational development outside school.   For
parents in the imperfect democracy there may be few such
opportunities.   They must resign themselves to seeing
their child moulded in all kinds of undesirable ways or,
more likely, simply turned off education in a noisy,
large, disruptive class where the teacher has little sense
of where the whole enterprise is going and is resigned
simply to attempting to 'keep order'.

I could continue to fill out this dilemma, adding in
various details which might seem to favour sticking with
the state system or withdrawing from it - things like how
much time the parents can spend on their children's education, how far the school is from realizing the aims of
education in a full-bodied democracy, and so on.   To do
so would be only to underline that we are faced here with
a moral dilemma, a clash of principles.   Whatever aspiring democrats do, they are likely to feel that they should
perhaps have taken the opposite course.   To support private schools goes against their beliefs about the place of
education in a democratic society, but to let their children endure an inadequate education is likely to affect
their development as morally responsible people.   Given
the context of the imperfect democracy I do not think it
is possible to provide any principles which will supply an
answer to this dilemma for all cases.   Like all such conflicts it can only be resolved in context, bearing certain
considerations in mind.   The prime considerations here
are: how bad is the education and in what ways exactly
and how remediable is the situation with the use of imagi-
nation and ingenuity?

Let me just indicate how I see these considerations
being applied.   If state schools are sexist or bent on
making religious converts it is probably possible in most
circumstances for committed democrats to combat these
influences.   If the state school is generally bad and in
many respects anti-educational, this may be more difficult, especially for busy and/or uneducated parents.   A

private school may have to be the answer.   This, I think,
is all one can say in general when faced with the situation of the individual parent in an imperfect democracy.
Unlike the fully-fledged democracy, where it is a matter
of establishing principles about the provision of education compatible with the aims of a democracy, with the
imperfect democracy it is a matter of individual choice in
many different kinds of imperfect situations which can
only be individually assessed bearing in mind certain
general considerations.   I am not saying of course that
such individual decisions cannot be critically examined
and held to be inadequately grounded, but only that one
cannot say, in general, that in an imperfect democracy it
is never, or always, a parent's duty to use private
schools when faced with inadequacies in the state educational system.

The conclusion to this lengthy consideration of whether
there are any parental rights as such is that there are
none.   Parents have no right to give their child sexist,
religious or indeed any kinds of education which impose a
particular conception of life upon her and attempt to
mould her into that conception.   If these arguments hold,
parents have no right to impose any particular conception
of life at all upon their children.   They may well have
manifold duties, and consequently some rights necessary
to the successful carrying out of the duties, but what
they do not have is rights qua parents which allow them
to direct their children's lives along certain particular
tracks.

CONCLUSIONS

This concluding section is subdivided into three parts.
The first two summarize conclusions reached on parental
duties and rights derived from these.   The third indicates the policy considerations which arise for a democratic community which takes this view of parental rights
and duties.

1   Parental duties in a democratic society

As we saw above parents' educational responsibilities can
be divided into two main categories.   (a) The first set
concerns those parts of the child's education which involve an intimate personal knowledge of her.   Early

learning of the mother tongue and early moral education
fall into this category.   (b) The second covers the
duties of monitor/co-ordinator of the child's educational
experiences.   The latter come from many sources and take
many different forms so the child needs help to enable
her to make something of herself and put together a
coherent education.   There is no necessity for this role
to be performed by parents and as children grow older it
will very likely be taken over in part by others to whom
the child may turn for advice.   In a society, however,
which is concerned that its members develop as morally
autonomous beings the performance of the role of monitor/
co-ordinator cannot be left to chance.   There may after
all be no one around at the crucial time prepared to offer
support and advice.   The society will assign this duty to
parents on the grounds that they are usually in the best
position to perform it and that given their natural interest in, and concern for, their children, they will want to
do so.   Not that in performing this duty parents will
eschew all help from others.   They will clearly be quite
prepared for their child to receive all kinds of advice
and support from others.   The point is simply that there
are people, parents, whose duty it is to see that the
child is being helped to integrate her educational experiences into a whole, whether they do it themselves, see it
in part being done by others - a sympathetic teacher, for
instance - or, increasingly, as she matures, by the child
herself.

This second set of parental duties to do with the inte-
gration of the child's educational experiences subdivides
into two specific responsibilities.   The first (b, i) is
that of intermediary between the child and the formal educational agencies.   Institutions are run on general
principles and even in the best of them an individual's
interests can slip through the mesh.   If, as well, the
institution is an educational one and the individual a
child, there needs to be someone to keep an eye on her
progress and well-being, e.g., to make sure that what she
is getting is making sense to her, that it is appropriate
to the stage she is at and that she is generally able to
take advantage of the opportunities offered by the institution to develop into an educated person.   As we saw
earlier parents are very well placed to take on these responsibilities.   They are in a position to have considerable understanding of, and insight into their child's
aspirations, inhibitions and interests and, as well, to be
the recipient of their child's confidences about difficulties at school, youth club or wherever.   Parents, then,

have a duty to mediate between the child and the educational institutions of which the child is a member.   Not that it will necessarily be the parents themselves who see the head, class teacher or subject specialist, since they may judge it best to encourage their child to take up the cudgels on her own behalf on some particular issue.   The point here, as I have stressed before, is that it is the parents' responsibility to make sure all is going smoothly.   How they set about tackling any hitches or difficulties will depend on their judgment of the specific situation and the kind of action called for.   Further, in the democratic society we have envisaged parents will not have to deal with such problems completely unaided.   There will be specific provision to help them to see if their children are getting all they should from the educational possibilities within the society and to provide them with advice about what to do in the case of any shortcomings (see section 3 below).

The second responsibility falling under the parents' monitoring/co-ordinating duties is (b, ii) helping to enrich their child's understanding of activities and perspectives on life beyond what can be provided by the basic education.   The orientation of the latter will be towards widening the child's awareness and appreciation of the activities one can indulge in and all the stances one can take to life.   For even the best planned and executed education can only be an opening-up.   Parents will need to encourage the investigation of further possibilities. In this they will be aided by the institutional support discussed in section 3 below.

These, then, are the broad duties assigned to parents in the democratic society envisaged.   To some readers they will seem tediously familiar.   They may claim with justice that this is exactly what good parents do in our society.   This is true and perhaps not surprising if it is the good practice of parents one has in mind.   The difference however between our society and the democratic society envisaged will become apparent when we consider the support (outlined in section 3 below) which is given to parents in performing their duties.

2 Parental rights in a democratic society

As we have seen there are no, so to speak, self-standing parental rights.   That is, there are no rights possessed by parents qua parents which permit them to direct their

children's lives along certain tracks.   In relation to
their child's education parents do, however, have two
sorts of rights.

(i) They have what I have referred to already as
'enabling rights'.   These are rights which enable them to
carry out the duties specified in the first section of
this conclusion.   Exactly what rights these are <u>in detail</u>
will depend on all kinds of contingent factors about the
society, its levels of wealth, education, technology and
so on.   There cannot, for instance, be rights of access
to computerized information in a society without such
hardware; but there may be rights to certain financial
provision to enable parents to carry out some duties.
Certainly there will be rights of access to all kinds of
information about one's own child's abilities and what
teachers say about her, and about the educational institutions themselves and the way they are run.   Such information is essential if parents are properly to do their job
as monitors/co-ordinators of their child's experiences.

(ii) Parents will also have the right, noted already, of
all citizens of a democratic society to interest others in
their hobbies, pastimes, concerns, with the normal provisos
about the appropriateness of the occasion, other people's
willingness to let themselves be interested, etc.   In
particular, they will have this right in respect of their
children.   Since children are involved, as well as the
usual provisos, there will be further qualifications limit-
ing this right with regard to the stage of the children's
moral development.   For instance, whilst it might be very
appropriate to introduce an adult foreign visitor to the
delights of a convivial evening spent in a British pub,
this would not be acceptable for a four-year-old child.

Also, as we have seen, parents have the right to raise
the question of whether their child should receive specialized training as a musician, gymnast, etc.   This is not
a right to determine that she shall have such a training,
the legal right which parents in our society have at the
moment.   It is only the right to raise the issue for discussion amongst relevant parties - teachers, coaches, the
child herself - so that the best course of action for the
child to safeguard her development as an autonomous person
can be instituted.

Although parents may have other rights (e.g. to do with
their responsibility for their child's more general well-
being and health) the above define the limits of their
rights in relation to their child's <u>educational</u> development.

3 The role of the community in relation to parents'
rights and duties: some policy considerations

(i) In the kind of democratic society outlined, the community will want to make provision for parents to fulfil
the duties set out in section 1 above.   This will involve
at least the following arrangements.

(a) Some form of parental education will need to be provided, for parents cannot perform their duties unless they
have knowledge and understanding of them.   A start can be
made on this in basic education for, as we shall see in
(c) below, it is important for non-parent citizens to be
acquainted with the general duties of parents, since they
will be called upon to support parents financially in
their duties through the public provision of certain
amenities.   All prospective citizens, then, will need
some awareness of the duties of a parent but parents and
prospective parents will need rather more extensive and
detailed provision.   This will cover matters to do with
mother tongue teaching, moral/political education and the
duties of parents as monitors/co-ordinators.   It could
well be seen as parallel to the professional training of
teachers in our society, particularly in-service training.

But, who, it might be asked, is going to set themselves
up to teach parents their job?   There are all kinds of
specialized knowledge found in educational studies for
teachers which would be just as useful to parents: knowledge to do with philosophical and psychological aspects
of concept learning or moral development for instance.
It simply is not the case that parents know these things
by the light of nature.   Reflective parents in our
society realize this, as is evidenced by the vast sales of
Dr Spock's, Hugh Jolly's books and so on.   As for the
machinery to be used, that will be a matter of detail for
a society to determine itself, by looking at other related
provision (perhaps, e.g., teacher training) and seeing how
this service for parents might be dovetailed in with it.

Should such parental education be compulsory?   A general orientation towards these duties will be included in
basic education.   What of more specialized provision?
There is perhaps little to be gained in making it compulsory.   From what we know of most parents' concern and
aspirations for their children, they will be keen to take
up what is on offer.   And after all, we do not have to
imagine a society making this provision in a slab-like
way, ten lectures for all prospective parents in the local

parish hall.   The provision can suit all temperaments and
learning styles.   There can be books, television programmes, radio programmes, discussion groups as an adjunct
of the local health clinic or schools, and so on.
Although there would be some machinery for drawing the
attention of parents to this provision, there would be
none compelling them to use it.   But citizens might well
want to make provision for more persuasive tactics with
failing, inadequate parents.   I take this up under (iii)
below.

(b) In addition to the provision of parental education,
designed to guide and inform parents about the performance
of their educational duties, the community will need to
make provision to enable parents adequately to perform
their monitoring role in relation to their child's education.   As we have seen, this has two aspects, each with
different implications for community policies.   Let us
first take the mediating aspect and its implications.
What changes in institutions and other kinds of support
are required to enable a parent to act as an intermediary
between his child and the formal educational agencies of
the society?   Schools, for instance, will have to adopt a
different attitude to parents from that adopted by many
today.   The appropriate attitude will be one that recognizes the parent as a co-operative partner in the educational enterprise.   Concretely, it will mean that all
kinds of information about curriculum policies and about
school organization will have to be made available to
parents and teachers will have to be prepared to discuss
with them the bearing of these policies on the life of
their child within the school.   For some matters at an
early stage, and for many matters at a late stage in a
child's education, it will be more appropriate for the
child, with parental advice and support, to discuss her
problems or suggestions with her teachers herself.
Learning to take responsibility for one's relations with
institutions is after all, an essential part of everyone's
education.   Whether the initiative is taken by the
parents or the child, or by both together, the same open,
positive attitude towards parents is required of the
school if parents are successfully to help their child to
get the best out of it.

It is a curious fact that many schools feel at the
moment that they have to adopt a defensive attitude
towards parental attempts to get information or to proffer
it.   It is especially curious when individual teachers
will often say how useful a chat with a parent at a

parents' evening has been in illuminating a child's attitude to a subject or in explaining some hitherto unex-
plainable piece of behaviour.   Presumably part of the
reason for the defensive attitude is the belief current in
our society that the teacher is the expert educator who
must not brook amateur meddling by non-experts.   Con-
scientious teachers with this belief would regard themselves as irresponsible if they let parents dictate pedagogical practices, just as a lawyer would regard himself
as irresponsible if he let a keen, legally inclined client
influence him on a point of law.   As the previous arguments about the nature of the parent's role show, however,
there is a place for parents' contributions.   Acting
within the bounds of his role, the parent is no officious
meddler.   The teacher has no grounds to reject all the
parents' requests for information, suggestions, etc. as
illegitimate.

   A teacher who accepts this re-drawing of the parental
role may still feel that it could not be implemented, on
the practical grounds that teachers just do not have
enough time to consult with parents about individual children on the scale that seems to be implied.   Without
specifying exactly how many hours of teacher-time this
would involve, one would speculate that it would be more
than the 15-20 minutes per parent per term usual, at best,
in the present system of parent/teacher evenings.   Any
more, overworked teachers will say, would be insupport-
able.   On this score, it seems to me, they would be
right.   British teachers at the moment work far longer
hours than their continental counterparts.   Indeed to
mention the hours the British teacher is expected to spend
in the classroom is to evoke gasps of horror from French,
German, Belgian colleagues at international conferences.
To pile on yet more hours of work would be unjust and
anti-educational: 'anti-educational' in that the educational enterprise requires time for reflection on its
proper conduct, if day-to-day classroom practice is not to
fall into the doldrums of habitual tasks - pages of sums,
French exercises, copying from reference books, etc. -
just because teachers have little time, and less mental
energy, to reflect on the fundamental aims of what they
are doing and how, concretely, these can best be realized.
To accommodate the necessary consultation with parents,
and because teachers already spend too much time in the
classroom than is good, educationally, for them and their
pupils, I would suggest a shortening of the school day.
This is in no sense a curtailing of education, quite the
opposite.   Absolutely necessary to solving some of its

most intractable problems, problems to do with pupils'
motivation and other reasons for failures to learn, is
setting aside time for parents and teachers to talk these
through.   Every teacher must have experienced the grati-
fying feeling of making a breakthrough with a child after
having reflected on why the child is not coping and possible reasons for her lack of interest, disruptive behaviour or whatever.   At the moment these experiences are
all too rare.   More time set aside for teacher reflection
and teacher/parent consultation might well increase them.
The same institutional openness as that displayed by the
school would have to be shown by youth clubs, Brownies,
Cubs, Scouts, and any other organization to which the
child might belong.   With respect to these, too, the
parent would have a mediating role to play and so would
need the same access to information, leaders' time, etc.

   If there is to be teacher/parent, parent/youth leader
consultation there will inevitably be disagreements at
times over what is best for the child.   Sometimes it will
be possible to talk these through and arrive at an agreed
solution.   Where it is not the society will need to have
some kind of independent educational Ombudsperson to step
in and resolve the matter.   There would probably be relatively few such cases, but clearly some kind of machinery
is necessary to cope with those that prove to be intractable.

(c)   Parents will also need support in that aspect of
their monitoring role which concerns the enriching of
their child's understanding of activities and perspectives on life which go beyond those available in basic
education.   Citizens will not want to leave provision
for this area as uneven as it is in our society.   They
will probably want to make considerable public provision
for children to pursue all kinds of interests, independently of parental financial, and other, support.   I am
thinking, for instance, of libraries, art galleries,
museums, swimming pools, sports centres, riding schools,
craft centres, science centres, theatre seats, concert
seats, opera seats which all young people, say up to the
age of 21, can use without payment.   Given their commitment to the development of morally autonomous citizens
such provision is a necessity, for if parents have to pay
for all the activities their child wants to explore, this
will impose a heavy financial burden on most of them.   It
will fall particularly heavily on those who have large
families and/or whose children are keen to explore costly
activities.   Even in a society without large income dif-

ferentials (see Chapter one) the cost of the extension of
basic education is still going to be intolerably high for
some parents.   Hence the need for public provision.
Citizens of a democratic society will be quite prepared
to spend their collective wealth like this because it will
be one way of trying to ensure that certain activities do
not become the prerogative of children of parents of certain social groups which would be quite opposed to the
general principles underlying a democratic society.

This point is independent of the issue of arts and
sports subsidies for adults in a democratic society.   As
Dworkin (1978b) and Ackerman (1980) have shown, there are
problems for liberals who want to argue that the government should support certain cultural activities, like
opera and ballet and so on, and, by implication, not
others like motorcycle racing.   For this is apparently to
suggest that the government should endorse one particular
set of values and that seems to contradict the very idea
of liberal democracy.   My argument leaves aside the question of whether or not the market approach is the right
one for adult citizens simply that a policy of free access
to cultural, sporting, scientific, etc. facilities for the
young is one which must be in the public interest for a
society of morally autonomous citizens.   In practice this
may sometimes mean a subsidy to sustain some little supported activity.   But the argument for this subsidy would
be a strictly educational one - based on the need for the
widest choice of options for individuals - and not one
based on the claim of a particular group that this activity is 'too valuable to be allowed to decline'.   As
Ackerman shows, in a related discussion of this point, the
educational argument is open to abuse.   It may be used to
protect objects that rank high in the value scheme of
groups who happen to be powerful at the moment.   But he
does suggest three guidelines which might be used to
inform 'good-faith judgment' in this area: (a) history:
the dominance of a value structure in the past which suggests that its re-emergence is a possibility;   (b) the
overall pattern of objects protected: this can be reviewed for bias towards the interests of powerful groups;
(c) simple passage of time: if a thousand years have
passed with no generation placing any intrinsic value on a
natural object, like, e.g., Niagara falls, perhaps objections to its use as a source of energy could be seriously
reviewed (Ackerman, 1980, pp. 216-17).   With further refinement on these lines the kind of argument needed to
support my case could be forthcoming.

However, is the educational case independent, practically speaking, of the question of subsidies for adults? What about the child who does not avail herself of the free offers, but only becomes interested in them later? There are two possible answers to this question.   It could be argued that it is the responsibility of parents, as we have seen, to bring these opportunities to the child's attention and, children being what they are, most of them will want to sample what is on offer, so the problem will not arise to any large extent.   Alternatively one could attempt to implement the same basic policy by the use of 'first-time-user vouchers' for these activities, usable by anyone at any age.   This could be cumbersomely bureaucratic and should probably only be entertained if the more administratively straightforward everything-free-to-21 proves in practice to be unfair to large numbers of individuals who are only interested in extending their basic education after they are 21.

Finally, to underline a point already made, this policy assumes a society with a certain level of wealth.   Not limitless wealth, because then the above problem would not arise, since subsidies could support all activities any citizen wanted to engage in; but sufficient wealth to make the subsidizing of these activities for the young (or first-time-users) a practicable policy.   But this, as we saw earlier, is not a straightforward empirical matter of inspecting the public coffers to see how much is available.   For what money is available for public interest policies (like this one) as against what is available for the private use of individuals will itself be an outcome of a political decision to apportion the total wealth of society in a particular way (see Chapter one, p. 31f).   There will, too, have to be a political judgment as to the amount that should be spent on extending educational options as distinct from the amount that should be spent on other public interest policies, like, e.g., defence. Any liberal democratic society will have to make these judgments which will necessarily be partly conditioned by historical factors.   The extension of educational activities, however, should have a high priority because after basic subsistence needs for food, shelter and defence of citizens have been attended to, this is a policy essential for the survival of democracy itself.

(ii) The discussion so far in this chapter has assumed, implicitly at least, that the exercise of parental rights and duties will take place within the conventional nuclear family.   Should we make this assumption, however, when we

know that in the UK one in three marriages break up and
that there are increasingly large numbers of one-parent
families?   We cannot.   Parental duties will obviously be
exercised in different family contexts and outside them.
This has a clear policy implication for a democratic
state.   On the one hand it will not interfere with citizens' personal and social relationships.   This would
drastically infringe their personal autonomy.   On the
other hand, in the interests of the developing autonomy of
its young citizens, the state will need to monitor the
social context in which parents perform their duties.   In
case this has a sinister ring, all that is intended is
that the community should attempt to investigate how far
the form of family life permits or militates against
parents fulfilling their educational duties.   In the
light of those investigations it will be the task of the
community to determine what should be done where parents
cannot perform their duties adequately.   To determine, in
other words, what changes could be made which would safeguard the autonomy both of the parents (to live out a certain life style) and of their children.

   It is not appropriate for me to attempt to outline the
kinds of machinery required for monitoring and support
since this case is pitched at the level of general principles and it will be for the democratic citizens to
determine these in their particular situation.   It is
enough to indicate that various levels of machinery will
be required for, e.g., investigation at the macro-societal
level as well as for intervention and help at the individual level.

(iii)   What, however, of parents who, despite the policies
of aid and support outlined under (i) and (ii) above, fall
short in their parental duties?   What does the democratic
society do about backsliding parents?   If this is due to
ignorance it can insist that they avail themselves of some
parental education.   Not, again, in a slab-like way, so
that they are prescribed ten weeks of such-and-such a
course;   but some provision might be prescribed appropriate to their particular failings.   If the failure is a
motivational one - they do not want to extend their
child's basic education or to monitor their child's relationship with the educational institution - then the only
recourse may be to give these responsibilities to some
other person, perhaps another family member, or a family
friend.   As we have seen before there is no reason why
some named person should not fill this newly designated
role of educational guardian in respect of these two

duties and why the child should not continue to live with
her parent(s), assuming that it is only these educational
duties which the parent(s) find irksome.   These duties,
after all, do not necessarily have to be performed by
parents.   But if the parents' distaste is for the duties
which must be performed by someone standing in a personal
relationship to the child (i.e., early mother tongue
teaching and moral education) then the child will have to
be put in the care of people willing and able to perform
them.

The solution to the problem of backsliding parents
depends very much, therefore, on the reason why they are
not performing their duties (is it ignorance or lack of
inclination?) and which duties they are not performing.
The solution must match the particular respect in which
the parent is falling short.

Conclusion

The last three chapters indicated ways in which a liberal democratic society might move beyond a dominatory struc- ture towards a participatory education system. Political education has a key role in this, reflected in its promi- nent position in this essay. The role of the headmaster, although unnecessary in the fully participatory democracy, can be used to transform schools into more democratic work-places for all their members. The role of parent, too, often regarded as a bulwark against the domination of the state or the teaching profession over the pupil, is seen in this essay as another power source which needs to be kept within appropriate bounds.

These three topics represent only a selection from the areas requiring attention in a move from a constitutional liberal democracy to a participatory system. Aside from the further work necessary on these three areas a number of other topics need to be tackled. I have restricted myself to basic education, but the area beyond this re- quires attention. What attitude should the participatory democracy take towards post-basic education? Should it hold fast to a distinction between professional education, i.e. the training required for jobs, both manual and non- manual, and education for personal development? Some might argue that whereas the moderately wealthy society considered here might maintain fairly strict controls over recruitment to the former to avoid imbalances between, e.g., ethnic groups and men and women represented in dif- ferent occupations, in the case of the latter it might allow equal freedom of access, for instance via a voucher system, to be used when the individual chooses. Is such a policy justifiable? It is not clear.

The role of research institutions in the participatory

democracy also requires investigation.   At the moment, in universities, teaching and research functions are usually combined.   It is not obvious that they should be or what kinds of control should be exercised over research.

Also, as I have said several times already, echoing Dworkin's plea for a liberal democratic theory of culture-support, the educational role of the media needs investigation in the light of work on freedom of expression in a liberal society and on bias.

These three areas are not unconnected.   But it must be left to another study to develop a framework within which rational and coherent policies for each of them can be worked out.

Notes

INTRODUCTION

1 Much of Kevin Harris's (1979) book for instance is a
convincing Marxist critique of current educational
practice. In its positive suggestions for 'anti-
education', however, we are not presented with any
well-worked out strategies for a change towards a more
desirable society.

> Anti-education can hardly be defined precisely at
> this point of time; but it would be a matter of
> people talking, acting and working informally among
> themselves; discussing their lives, their freedoms,
> their constraints, their situations, their visions
> and their knowledge of the world; discovering the
> world for themselves through experience and with
> authorities, and linking up with movements in other
> areas of society, in a gradual process of changing
> themselves, education and society. It would seek
> out new forms, new goals, new directions, new pro-
> cesses and new social relations for the transmission
> and assimilation of knowledge; and in so doing it
> would have to continually recreate its research pro-
> gramme as it sought, adopted and promoted new and,
> (hopefully) undistorted ways of seeing the world
> (Harris, 1979, p. 188).

Harris gives a number of reasons why we 'should not
realistically expect a rush on anti-education' (Harris,
1979, p. 188). These are connected, for the most
part, with the stakes which people have in the status
quo. Another reason, however, for any reluctance
which people might show in taking up 'anti-education'
is that it is unclear what one should do and how success might be measured.

171

I have tried to suggest a number of possible ways forward to a less dominatory society, including suggestions for political education, a changed role for headteachers and so on.   I do not claim that these are 'the answers' but they are specific concrete policies to be considered on their merits.

2   I recognize that on the way to a participatory democracy from a society like our own there may well have to be preferential policies, or policies of reverse discrimination, where women are treated differently from men.   The same would be true for other groups in the population, e.g., blacks,,who have been unjustifiably discriminated against in the past.   I do not argue for these in this book as I am concerned to discuss other policies to achieve an equitable distribution of power. I would support such policies, however, on the grounds, which Dworkin does in 'Reverse Discrimination' (Dworkin, 1977).

3   I am thinking here of Carole Pateman (1970, 1979) and Amy Gutmann (1980).

CHAPTER 1   DEMOCRATIC PRINCIPLES AND BASIC ASSUMPTIONS

1   See Benn (1976) for the notion of a person on which my account relies.

2   See Hart (1961, pp. 189-95) for an elaboration of this account of the normal human person.

3   For an exposition and development of this position in relation to the aims of education see John White (1982).

4   In Chapter two I attempt to give an account of the fraternal attitude which should obtain between citizens in a democratic community.   This supplements the account of the democratic citizen sketched here.   It cannot be spelt out at this stage because it would anticipate the treatment of participatory democracy at the end of this present chapter.

5   The example is Ronald Dworkin's (1977, p. 234ff).

6   For instance, Oppenheim (1981, pp. 22-3), Peters (1967, p. 93) and Lukes (1977, p. 32) distinguish between the concepts of authority and power in different ways, indicating at the same time that other drawings of the conceptual map in this area for other purposes could be acceptable.

CHAPTER 2   REALIZING DEMOCRATIC PRINCIPLES: INSTITUTIONS
AND ATTITUDES

1   There are, however, some elements of the machinery sug-
    gested here in the Yugoslav system of self-management
    and in the Mondragon co-operatives of the Spanish
    Basque country.   (See, e.g., Oakeshott, 1978, Chapter
    10.)
2   This is also the view of Ronald Dworkin who says, 'it
    will be impossible to devise political procedures that
    will accurately discriminate between personal and ex-
    ternal preferences' (Dworkin, 1977).   I do not know if
    Dworkin would think that there is anything in Pennock's
    idea of the 'quantum of votes', which I discuss.   It
    clearly does not guarantee accuracy in discrimination
    but it may none the less be a useful device in some
    situations.
3   See, e.g., Barry, 1965, Note B, and 1973; Weiss,
    1973(a) and 1973(b); Pennock, 1974.
4   I have not discussed the idea of 'consociational demo-
    cracy' (see Barry, 1979 and the references in that
    article in note 24) since, the solution of taking
    minorities into the government as equal partners, is
    one which has been developed for representative democ-
    racies.   The focus of my interest here has been parti-
    cipatory democracy.   As a way of coping with the
    minority problem in a situation in which representation
    is necessary there seems much to be said for the con-
    sociational solution.
5   I do not discuss the conscription case since this
    raises further issues which I do not want to develop
    here.   In a different context I would want to raise
    the question of whether a policy of conscription is
    ever justified.
6   For discussions of definitional and substantive issues
    to do with civil disobedience, see, e.g., Bedau, 1969;
    Held, Nielsen and Parsons (eds), 1972, Part Two; Hon-
    derich, 1980, Chapter three; Rawls, 1972, Chapter VI,
    sections 53-9; Singer, 1973.
7   'Constitutional democracy' is a useful term used by a
    former doctoral student of mine, Dr Michael Zlotnik, in
    his thesis, to describe states which have a democratic
    constitutional structure (e.g., elections, legal oppo-
    sition parties, procedures for fair trials, etc.) but
    where other social arrangements (e.g., authority struc-
    tures in the work-place) are not democratically organ-
    ized.
8   I am thinking here of work I have referred to before in
    this essay by, e.g., Bok, 1978; Dworkin, 1977; Hon-
    derich, 1980; Passmore, 1974; Singer, 1979.

CHAPTER 3   POLITICAL EDUCATION

1   I am well aware of the sketchy nature of the first sec-
    tion of this chapter.   It leaves many issues undiscus-
    sed and unargued.   It is intended, however, only to
    provide a background to some of the points made about
    the relationship between political education and the
    formal organization of education later in this chapter.

    In a fuller treatment, for instance, I would need to
    say more at this point about the possible forms which
    the organization of education at local level might
    take.   In an earlier draft I attempted to do this but
    it made this section complicated and unwieldy without
    adding substantially to the main argument about the
    necessary interconnections between political education
    and the organization of education - whatever particular
    form the latter takes.
2   See the next main section of this chapter, Political
    education in a participatory democracy, for a spelling
    out of the main outlines of the political education re-
    ferred to here.
3   I do not think political education is ruled out in the
    first school by the problem of indoctrination because
    as I have indicated here (see p. 109f) and elsewhere
    (White, 1977, pp. 52-4) I do not think there need be
    such a problem.
4   This suggestion for a political education element in
    professional training programmes should not be viewed
    in isolation.   In so far as there was such an ele-
    ment, this should increase the chances of success of
    the co-ordinated 'politics across the curriculum poli-
    cies' advocated earlier.

CHAPTER 4   HEADTEACHERS: A CHANGING ROLE

1   The proposals here about the content of the heads'
    training programmes overlap with the proposals for the
    content of the more general professional training pro-
    grammes advocated in Chapter three.   This degree of
    repetition seemed to me unavoidable since some users of
    this book might be interested in one policy rather than
    the other and would find it useful to have all the
    relevant material in one place.
2   I should point out that this course did not have as its
    focus a consideration of what would be involved in run-
    ning a school along democratic lines, although its
    participants chose this topic for discussion.

CHAPTER 5   PARENTS' EDUCATIONAL RIGHTS AND DUTIES

1   There is now an extensive literature on rights.   Colin
    Wringe's (1981) bibliography is an excellent source of
    books and papers in political philosophy on rights.
    For anyone interested in general issues to do with
    rights it could profitably be consulted in conjunction
    with Wringe's useful review of different kinds of
    rights and their justifications (Wringe, 1981, parts II
    and III).   The same book also discusses children's
    rights in particular.   For a brief, readable overview
    of the main issues concerning education and rights, see
    Snook and Lankshear (1979).
2   D.W. Hamlyn (1978, pp. 130-1) makes a similar distinc-
    tion.

Bibliography

The bibliography lists only books and papers referred to
in the text.

Ackerman, B. (1980), Social Justice in the Liberal State,
  New Haven and London, Yale University Press.
Bachrach, P. and Baratz, M.S. (1970), Power and Poverty.
  Theory and Practice, New York, Oxford University Press.
Barry, B. (1965), Political Argument, London, Routledge &
  Kegan Paul.
Barry, B. (1973), 'Wollheim's Paradox: Comment' in Politi-
  cal Theory, vol. I, no. 3, August.
Barry, B. (1979), 'Is Democracy Special?' in P. Laslett
  and J. Fishkin (eds), Philosophy, Politics and Society
  (Fifth Series), Oxford, Basil Blackwell.
Bedau, H.A. (ed.) (1969), Civil Disobedience, New York,
  Pegasus.
Benn, S.I. (1976), 'Freedom, Autonomy and the Concept of
  a Person' in Proceedings of the Aristotelian Society,
  vol. 76.
Benton, T. (1982), 'Realism, Power and Objective Inter-
  ests' in K. Graham (ed.), Contemporary Political Philo-
  sophy, Cambridge University Press.
Blumberg, P. (1968), Industrial Democracy: The Sociology
  of Participation, London, Constable.
Boggs, C. (1976), Gramsci's Marxism, London, Pluto Press.
Bok, S. (1978), Lying: Moral Choice in Public and Private
  Life, Hassocks, Sussex, Harvester Press.
Braverman, H. (1974), Labour and Monopoly Capital, New
  York, Monthly Review Press.
Bullock, Lord (1977), Report of the Committee of Inquiry
  on Industrial Democracy, London, HMSO.
Clegg, H. (1951), Industrial Democracy and Nationalisation,
  Oxford, Basil Blackwell.

Clegg, H. (1960), A New Approach to Industrial Democracy,
    Oxford, Basil Blackwell.
Cohen, B. (1978), 'Equality, Freedom and Independent
    Schools', Journal of Philosophy of Education, vol. 12.
Cole, G.D.H. (1917), Self-Government in Industry, London,
    Hutchinson.
Cole, G.D.H. (1918), 'Recent Developments in the British
    Labour Movement', American Economic Review, September.
Cole, G.D.H. (1920), Guild Socialism Restated, London,
    Leonard Parsons.
Connell, R.W. (1971), The Child's Construction of Politics,
    Melbourne University Press.
Crenson, M.A. (1971), The Un-Politics of Air Pollution: A
    Study of Non-Decision-making in the Cities, Baltimore
    and London, The John Hopkins Press.
Crick, B. and Porter, A. (eds) (1978), Political Education
    and Political Literacy, London, Longmans.
Dahl, R.A. (1956), A Preface to Democratic Theory,
    University of Chicago Press.
Dahl, R.A. (1961), Who Governs? Democracy and Power in an
    American City, New Haven and London, Yale University
    Press.
Dahl, R.A. (1970), After the Revolution?, New Haven and
    London, Yale University Press.
Dunlop, F. (1979), 'On the Democratic Organisation of
    Schools', Cambridge Journal of Education, vol. I,
    no. 9.
Dworkin, R. (1977), Taking Rights Seriously, London,
    Duckworth.
Dworkin, R. (1978a), 'Philosophy and Politics' in B.
    Magee (ed.), Men of Ideas, London, BBC.
Dworkin, R. (1978b), 'Liberalism' in S. Hampshire (ed.),
    Public and Private Morality, Cambridge University Press.
Edgley, R. (1978), 'Education for Industry', Radical
    Philosophy, Spring.
Edgley, R. (1980), 'Education, work and politics', Journal
    of Philosophy of Education, 14.
Ekholm, M. (1977), School Leader Education in Sweden,
    Report no. 1.
Giddens, A. (1979), Central Problems in Social Theory,
    London, Macmillan.
Graham, K. (ed.) (1982), Contemporary Political Philosophy,
    Cambridge University Press.
Gramsci, A. (1971), Selections from Prison Notebooks,
    London, Lawrence & Wishart.
Greenstein, F.I. (1965), Children and Politics, New Haven
    and London, Yale University Press.
Gutmann, A. (1980), Liberal Equality, Cambridge University
    Press.

Habermas, J. (1976), Legitimation Crisis, London, Heine-
    mann.
Hamlyn, D.W. (1978), Experience and the Growth of Under-
    standing, London, Routledge & Kegan Paul.
Harris, K. (1979), Education and Knowledge, London, Rout-
    ledge & Kegan Paul.
Hart, H.L.A. (1961), The Concept of Law, Oxford University
    Press.
Heater, D. (1977), 'International Studies at School level:
    the findings of recent British research' in Crick, B.
    and Heater, D., Essays on Political Education, The
    Falmer Press.
Hegel, G.W.F. (1942), Hegel's Philosophy of Right, trans-
    lated by T.M. Knox, Oxford, Clarendon Press.
Held, V., Nielsen, K. and Parsons, C. (eds) (1972), Philo-
    sophy and Political Action, New York, Oxford University
    Press.
Hill, S.B. (1979), 'Self-Determination and Autonomy' in
    R. Wasserstrom (ed.), Today's Moral Problems, 2nd edn,
    New York and London, Macmillan.
Hirsch, F. (1977), Social Limits to Growth, London, Rout-
    ledge & Kegan Paul.
Honderich, T. (1980), Violence for Equality: Inquiries in
    Political Philosophy, Harmondsworth, Penguin Books.
Johnson, N. et al. (1970), 'The Relationship between Chil-
    dren's Preferences For and Knowledge about other
    Nations', in British Journal of Social and Clinical
    Psychology, 9.
Kolakowski, L. (1978), Main Currents of Marxism, Oxford
    University Press.
Lukes, S. (1973), Individualism, Oxford, Blackwell.
Lukes, S. (1974), Power: A Radical View, London, Macmillan.
Lukes, S. (1977), Essays in Social Theory, London, Mac-
    millan.
Macpherson, C.B. (1977), The Life and Times of Liberal
    Democracy, Oxford University Press.
MacRae, D.G. (1969), 'Karl Marx' in T. Raison (ed.), The
    Founding Fathers of Social Science, Harmondsworth,
    Penguin.
Michael, J. (1982), The Politics of Secrecy, Harmonds-
    worth, Penguin.
Mill, J.S. (1910), Utilitarianism, Liberty and Representa-
    tive Government, London, J.M. Dent & Sons, Everyman
    Library.
Miller, D. (1977), 'Socialism and the Market', Political
    Theory, November.
Nagel, T. (1978), 'Ruthlessness in Public Life' in Hamp-
    shire, S. (ed.), Public and Private Morality, Cambridge
    University Press.

Nozick, R. (1974), Anarchy, State and Utopia, Oxford,
   Blackwell.
Nyberg, D. (1981), Power over Power, Ithaca and London,
   Cornell University Press.
Oakeshott, R. (1978), The Case for Workers' Co-ops, Rout-
   ledge & Kegan Paul.
Oppenheim, F. (1981), Political Concepts, Oxford, Basil
   Blackwell.
Passmore, J. (1974), Man's Responsibility for Nature,
   London, Duckworth.
Pateman, C. (1970), Participation and Democratic Theory,
   Cambridge University Press.
Pateman, C. (1979), The Problem of Political Obligation,
   Chichester, John Wiley & Sons.
Pennock, J.R. (1974), 'Democracy is not Paradoxical: Com-
   ment', Political Theory, vol. I, no. 4, February.
Pennock, J.R. (1979), Democratic Political Theory, Prince-
   ton University Press.
Peters, R.S. (1967), 'Authority' in A. Quinton (ed.),
   Political Philosophy, Oxford University Press.
Rawls, J. (1972), A Theory of Justice, Oxford University
   Press.
Richards, J.R. (1980), The Sceptical Feminist, London,
   Routledge & Kegan Paul.
Robins, L.J. and V.M. (1978), 'Politics in the First
   School: This Year, Next Year, Sometime ... Never?',
   Teaching Politics, vol. 7, no. 3.
Schumpeter, J. (1976), 5th edn, Capitalism, Socialism and
   Democracy, London, Allen & Unwin.
Singer, P. (1973), Democracy and Disobedience, London,
   Oxford University Press.
Singer, P. (1979), Practical Ethics, Cambridge University
   Press.
Snook, O. and Lankshear, C. (1979), Education and Rights,
   Melbourne University Press.
Sockett, H. (ed.) (1980), Accountability in the English
   Educational System, London, Hodder & Stoughton.
Stevens, O. (1982), Children Talking Politics: Political
   Learning in Childhood, Oxford, Martin Robertson.
Tajfel, H. (1966), 'Children and Foreigners' in New
   Society, 7.
Thomas, R. (1978), The British Philosophy of Administra-
   tion, London, Longman.
Tucker, D.F.B. (1980), Marxism and Individualism, Oxford,
   Basil Blackwell.
Verba, S. and Nie, N.N. (1972), Participation in America,
   New York, Harper & Row.
Verba, S., Nie, N.N. and Kim, J.O. (1971), The Modes of
   Democratic Participation: A Cross-National Comparison,
   Beverly Hills.

Warnock, M. (1977), Schools of Thought, London, Faber.

Weiss, D. (1973a), 'Wollheim's Paradox: Survey and Solution', Political Theory, vol. I, no. 2, May.

Weiss, D. (1973b), 'Rejoinder' (to Barry, 1973), Political Theory, Vol. I, no. 3, August.

White, J.P. (1982), The Aims of Education Restated, London, Routledge & Kegan Paul.

White, John and White, Pat (1976), 'A Programme for Political Education: a Critique', Teaching Politics, vol. 5, no. 3.

White, Pat (1973), 'Education, Democracy and the Public Interest', in R.S. Peters (ed.), The Philosophy of Education, London, Oxford University Press.

White, Pat (1977), 'Political Education in a Democracy: The Implications for Teacher Education', Journal of Further and Higher Education, vol. I, no. 3.

Williams, B. (1962), 'The Idea of Equality' in P. Laslett and W.G. Runciman (eds), Philosophy, Politics and Society (Second Series), Oxford, Basil Blackwell.

Williams, B. (1973), 'A Critique of Utilitarianism', in J.J.C. Smart and B. Williams, Utilitarianism For and Against, Cambridge University Press.

Williams, B. (1978), 'Politics and Moral Character', in S. Hampshire (ed.), Public and Private Morality, Cambridge University Press.

Willis, P. (1977), Learning to Labour, Westmead, Saxon House.

Wollheim, R. (1962), 'A Paradox in the Theory of Democracy', in P. Laslett and W.G. Runciman (eds), Philosophy, Politics and Society (Second Series), Oxford, Basil Blackwell.

Wright, A.W. (1979), G.D.H. Cole and Socialist Democracy, Oxford University Press.

Wringe, C.A. (1981), Children's Rights: A Philosophical Study, London, Routledge & Kegan Paul.

Index